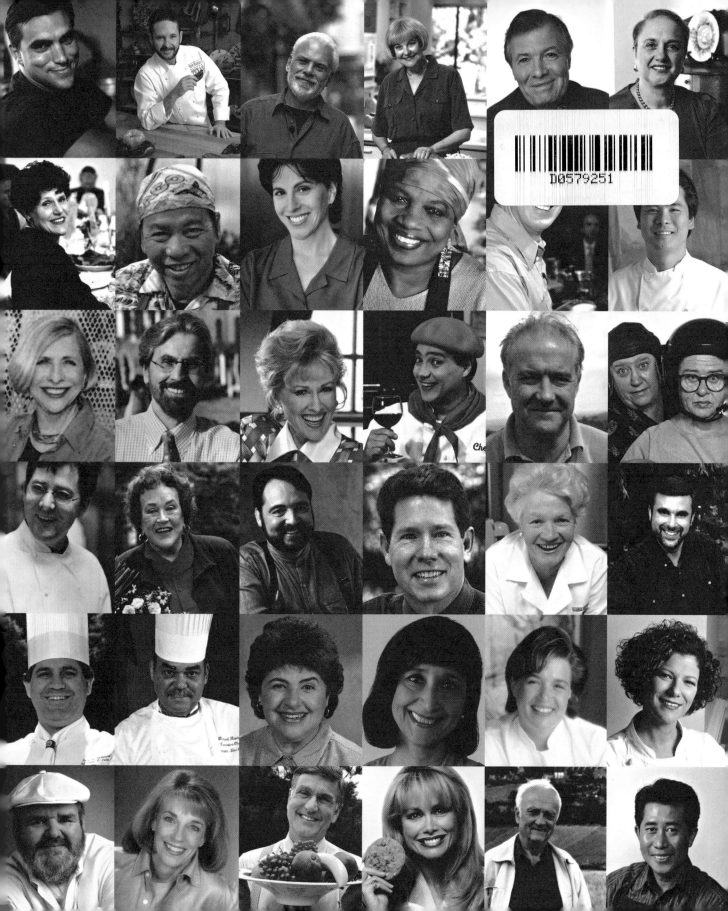

# AN AMERICAN

# *feast*

A Celebration of Cooking on Public Television

# AN AMERICAN *feast*

*foreword by Julia Child*

## A Celebration of Cooking on Public Television

Companion to the public television feast hosted by Julia Child and Burt Wolf
With chefs Martin Yan, Lidia Matticchio Bastianich, Paul Prudhomme, Jacques Pépin, and Nathalie Dupree

**BAY**
BOOKS

*San Francisco*

A LaCarte
COMMUNICATIONS

This book is published to accompany the program
*An American Feast*. This program is a production of
A La Carte Communications.

Bay Books is an imprint of Bay Books & Tapes, Inc.,
555 De Haro St., No. 220, San Francisco, CA  94107.

Managing Editor: Jane Horn
Cover and Book Design: Intersection Studio
Proofreader: Virginia Simpson-Magruder
Indexer: Elizabeth Parson
Photographer: Joyce Oudkerk Pool
Food Stylist: Pouké
Prop Stylist: Carol Hacker at Tabletop Prop
Photo Assistant: Arjen Kammeraad
Food Stylist Assistant: Jeff Tucker

Library of Congress Cataloging-in-Publication Data

An American Feast: a celebration of cooking on public television.
    p. cm.
  "Over 100 of the best recipes from public televisions favorite
chefs. Based on the public television feast hosted by Julia Child
and Burt Wolf, with chefs Martin Yan, Lidia Matticchio
Bastianich, Paul Prudhomme, Jacques Pépin, and Nathalie
Dupree [A La Carte Communications]."
  Includes index.
  ISBN 1-57959-502-2
  1. Cookery, American.
TX715.T21263  1999
641.5973—dc21
                                            99-37554
                                            CIP

ISBN 1-57959-502-2

Printed in China

10 9 8 7 6 5 4 3 2 1

Distributed by Publishers Group West

# Contents

## I22 DESSERTS AND BREADS
with Nathalie Dupree

# Foreword

BY JULIA CHILD

Cooking on television began for me on February 11, 1962, based on my first cookbook, *Mastering the Art of French Cooking*. I was invited to the studio of Boston's new educational television station, WGBH, to participate in an experiment: a how-to television program called *The French Chef*. From there, perhaps because we all had so much fun working together, teaching people to cook on television became a way of life. I would not exist at all were it not for public television. And I will be forever grateful to it for providing me with this opportunity.

Our first show was recorded as an experiment, on second-hand tape. Did people really want a cooking show? It turned out they did.

Did they really want French cooking? They did!

The Kennedys were in the White House, and their every move was news. They had that great French chef, René Verdon. French cooking was *in*. You could finally get to Europe in a few hours by air rather than taking almost a week by sea. People came back and they wanted to have some of that wonderful food, right here in the USA.

Our timing was right—two or three years earlier and we'd have laid an egg. Now, nearly thirty-eight years later, I'm still right here on public television, and now joined by dozens of other cooks, chefs, and cooking teachers who reach out to almost 100 million homes, nourishing what now seems like an insatiable hunger for "More Food!" Who would have been prescient enough to envision the public's evolution in appetite and taste, both at the table and on the tube. This volume of *An American Feast*, and the public television special that accompanies it, is present and tangible proof of the positive power of educational television to reach huge numbers of people with programming that was not seen as viable or profitable for commercial television. Yet public television's cooking shows ended up profoundly influencing some very basic ways we now live and eat at our century's end.

I have always done things my way, and working with public television gave me an open forum—PBS never put a crimp in my style, or that of my colleagues. It never dictated how much butter I could use, or for that matter how much garlic Jacques

Pépin put in his stuffing, or how little fat Graham Kerr should use. We could never have this kind of freedom to be who we are, and whip up what we want to, on commercial television.

Let's look at what's been cooking on public TV. My co-host Burt Wolf has shared travel and dining tips, expanding the culinary wish lists of millions of viewers. Jacques Pépin's mastery of cooking techniques has awed and inspired cooks for years, motivating many to study cooking and gastronomy formally, some even becoming professional chefs. Lidia Bastianich has shared her Istrian childhood and Italian family table with us, opening windows to culture and community along with cuisine. Paul Prudhomme and Nathalie Dupree let us know how much good cooking happens right in our own back-yard, and Martin Yan's mastery of wok and cleaver show us how much pleasure we can get from looking beyond our backyard, especially when he takes us on the road with him. Pierre Franey took us to France, the Frugal Gourmet to Italy, Roy Yamaguchi to Hawaii, Stephan Pyles to the "New Texas," Justin Wilson to good old Louisiana, and Marcia Adams right back to the "Heartland." "And Julia?" you may ask. I have had the great privilege of inviting you into my kitchen to cook with me and with many of the top chefs and bakers in America. Many of the new generation of master chefs grew up watching public television and were inspired to their current careers by watching *Today's Gourmet* and *The Galloping Gourmet* as well as *The French Chef* and many of our other shows on their PBS stations.

Of course, I could go on, but our family of public television chefs, and some of their favorite recipes, make a stronger statement as to why and how cooking has become so beloved by our audiences, and why, as we head into the next millennium, wishing someone *bon appétit* in the United States takes on a whole new meaning and appreciation.

*Bon appétit!*

# Acknowledgments

This book, and the three-hour public television program to which it is a companion, required contributions from dedicated professionals across the country. Without their efforts and willingness to participate there would not have been this gastronomic celebration for the new century.

Of course, the heart of the project consists of our hosts, Julia Child and Burt Wolf, and our five chefs, Martin Yan, Lidia Matticchio Bastianich, Paul Prudhomme, Jacques Pépin, and Nathalie Dupree. Their superb talents in the kitchen and teaching skills in front of the camera are matched by their meticulous recipe writing. In addition, more than two dozen public television cooks graciously allowed us to use excerpts from their programs and to reprint some of their best recipes in this commemorative book.

Behind the scenes we were privileged to have an incomparable staff. Susie Heller coordinated the feast and the recipes you find here, delivering the impossible—or at least improbable—in time for every deadline. Theresa Statz was everywhere, dealing with chefs, publishers, and television technicians with intelligence and diligence that cannot be surpassed. Geneva Collins provided our insightful opening chapter and met a deadline few writers can even contemplate. Lonnie Porro made the complex television event happen with her usual skill and imperturbable charm. And there were dozens of others operating cameras and word processors, designing sets and page layout, getting the groceries and cleaning up afterward.

The idea and support for *An American Feast* came from within public television. Kent Steele of Georgia Public Television first brought the project to us. Alan Foster and Allison White of the Public Broadcasting Service and Joe Zesbaugh of American Public Television provided the spiritual and financial support we needed. This was probably the first major collaboration between the two organizations. BaBette Davidson of GPTV, DeAnne Hamilton and Peter Calabrese of KQED, David Othmer of WHYY, Randy Feldman and Beth Utterback of WYES, and Beth Courtney of Louisiana Public Television helped us create a live national link-up to present the feast. Thanks, too, go to the producers, directors, technicians, and kitchen staffs at all those stations. At Bay Books, James Connolly's vision and the editorial efforts of Clancy Drake, Beth Weber, and Jane Horn produced this book in about a third of the time usually needed to publish a cookbook of this caliber. You all have our undiluted thanks.

An extra, and special, mention must be made of the contributions of Julia Child. It has been our honor and privilege to work with this remarkable woman for almost a decade. Along with everything else she is doing for public television and its viewers, Julia gave unsparingly of her time, effort, and considerable insight to make this project a success.

Finally, here's to you! *An American Feast* celebrates not only more than three decades of cooking on public television—the programs and the cooks. It also celebrates the change in the American palate, a change reflected in every part of the country and across all categories of individuals. Without you, this book and the public television programs on which it is based would not exist.

Geoffrey Drummond and Natan Katzman
A La Carte Communications

# Introduction

## OUR INSATIABLE APPETITE FOR TV COOKS

In the beginning, there was black and white Julia, all six feet two inches of her, in a makeshift kitchen in the back of a utility company's auditorium, a few pots and pans, and two cameras. She whisked eggs with passion, poured them into a pan, and an omelet materialized before our eyes. We were mesmerized, and a star was born.

That 1962 pilot of *The French Chef* was public television's first foray into the arena of cooking shows. More than three decades later Julia Child is still in the kitchen as cameras roll, but if you assembled the lineup of chefs on public television channels around the country in one gigantic kitchen, you could feed the passenger list of the *Queen Elizabeth 2*.

Just what is it about public television and the cooking show format that has proved such a delectable and time-tested recipe?

Let us begin with Julia, who is never called by her last name. The woman who was neither French nor a chef made her first appearance on educational television (as it was called in its early days) in 1962 on a book program produced by station WGBH in Boston. Promoting her first book, *Mastering the Art of French Cooking*, which she had published a few months before with French colleagues Simone Beck and Louisette Bertholle, Julia brought eggs, a whisk, a copper bowl, and a hot plate to demonstrate omelet making because she didn't know how she could fill up her allotted interview time with just talk. Her appearance generated a flurry of letters and gave WGBH producers Ruth Lockwood and Russell Morash the idea to do the pilot for what would

become *The French Chef*. (The title was not Julia's, who has always called herself a home cook. It was chosen because it fit on one line in TV program guides.)

*The French Chef* ran from 1963 to 1966 (in black and white) and 1970 to 1973 (in color), comprising more than 200 episodes. Not only were they shown in endless reruns at the time, they have resurfaced in the '90s on cable TV's Food Network, introducing a whole new generation to Julia's ebullient personality, her unflappability in the wake of kitchen disasters, and her genuine passion for cooking. She was not TV's first cook—a cooking school/restaurant owner named Dione Lucas and the legendary James Beard, among countless others, had programs on commercial television—but she has proved to be the most enduring. It was Morash's vision, in an age when his commercial counterparts were already sizing up TV talent by hairstyles, orthodontia, and poise, to point the camera at a fifty-year-old self-described "housewife in sneakers" with no professional acting experience and that trilling, breathy, clearly untrained voice. In public television, then as now, substance was not sacrificed for style, and Julia knew her French cooking. The Cordon Bleu graduate had spent ten years testing and re-testing the recipes that went into *Mastering the Art of French Cooking*. She knew American kitchens and American supermarkets, and she sensed that Americans were ready for something more than TV dinners and can-opener cuisine.

"The unique blend of Julia's earthy humor and European sophistication, her tendency to slap and sniff and taste everything without losing a shred of dignity, were there from the beginning," *The New Yorker* wrote in a glowing profile in 1974. "In a sense, she offered 'snobbery made easy' by combining a plummy accent and a love of French food with a typically American do-it-yourself approach," Laurence Jarvik wrote of Julia's long-lasting appeal in his 1997 book, *PBS: Behind the Screen*.

In those early days, cooking shows were shot as one continuous take (re-shooting and splicing the tape were too expensive and time-consuming). Part of the charm of *The French Chef* is watching Julia's aplomb and inventiveness in the wake of aspics that wouldn't unmold, flambés that wouldn't flame, and charlottes that collapsed on their way to the table. A few myths debunked: she never dropped a chicken (or fish or leg of lamb) on the floor, as is often cited (it was a potato pancake, which fell on the counter, out of camera view), and she didn't tipple wine as she cooked. (The "wine" in the bottle in the scenes presenting the finished dishes was really Gravy Master, according to Noël Riley Fitch, author of Julia's 1997 biography, *Appetite for Life*.)

Julia's rampant success inspired public television (the public broadcasting system was officially christened in 1967) to launch other TV cooks in the '70s. Joyce Chen, owner of New England's first Mandarin Chinese restaurant, taught viewers how to adapt Chinese cooking to American kitchens in *Joyce Chen Cooks*. Similarly, shows like *The Romagnolis' Table* opened the eyes of an increasingly sophisticated dining public, in this case, to a world of Italian eat-

ing beyond spaghetti and tomato sauce. Although he was a couple of decades away from making his public television debut, Graham Kerr splashed on the scene as *The Galloping Gourmet*, a Canadian-produced series, in 1969. Serious foodies dismissed his sloppy techniques, but viewers adored his saucy wit during his three-year reign. He promoted the idea that cooking should be fun, which was good for the genre as a whole. Julia herself continued to make shows for WGBH in the late '70s and early '80s: *Julia Child & Company*, *Julia Child & More Company*, and *Dinner at Julia's*.

Enter the 1980s, the era that spawned the word "yuppie," turned noodles into "pasta," and gave Americans a taste for goat cheese and pesto. A funky little Berkeley restaurant that focused on organic cuisine, Chez Panisse, was elevated to a Temple of Gastronomy. Wolfgang Puck topped a pizza with smoked salmon and crème fraîche at Spago, his L.A. restaurant. Donald Trump made conspicuous consumption seem like a patriotic duty. On public television's airwaves, cooking shows were propagating faster than morels in April rains to take advantage of America's expanding curiosity about the provenance of regional dishes, ethnic flavors, and artisanal techniques.

The cooking show itself was changing, too. The creators of these programs began to recognize that although there would always be a dedicated cadre of fans who would watch with bechamel-splattered loose-leaf notebook in hand, copying down ingredients and procedures that would be translated into

Saturday night dinner, there were legions of folks who didn't know a pastry blender from a potato ricer who tuned in for sheer entertainment. (There is after all, a magician-like quality to taking raw, run-of-the-mill ingredients and transforming them into an ethereal thing of beauty, ready to disappear forever at the plunge of a fork.) The strict instructional format, a comfort to a medium devoted to educational programming, was loosened up to make cooking shows more *fun* to look at. Cooking shows became less about recipe recitations than about demonstrating techniques and explaining the history and lore of a dish. And there was always the companion cookbook (and a decade later, the web site) for the serious cook if he or she needed to know how many tablespoons of flour went into the soufflé.

Many of the TV chefs still around today got their start in this era. Martin Yan, whose *Yan Can Cook* first aired in 1982, wowed crowds with his flashy cleaver work (he could debone a chicken in under twenty seconds and staged races with other chefs at chopping tasks) and outrageous puns ("school of hard woks"). Sure, he was a serious chef who had graduated from the prestigious Overseas Institute of Cookery in Hong Kong and had run his own cooking school, but it was showmanship that got him on the air. Many a home cook probably keeps a jar of hoisin sauce or bok choy in the refrigerator today because Martin demystified the ingredients. Justin Wilson, the wily Cajun humorist who can perhaps lay claim to being the most colorful cook on the airwaves, also began his *Louisiana Cookin'* shows in the '80s. (A 1989

piece in *Vogue* focusing on Justin said that in the white bread world of television the only true eccentrics are found on public television cooking shows.) Maybe his fans never tried his recipes for alligator or crawfish, but he was a goodwill ambassador for his state and certainly helped introduce hot peppers and filé gumbo (as well as his trademark phrase "I guar-ON-tee") to the nation.

The mantle of French cooking, meanwhile, was being passed on to others, including Madeleine Kamman, Pierre Franey, and Jacques Pépin, who continued Julia's mission of making Gallic techniques and methods accessible to Americans. As food tastes and restaurant experiences grew ever more refined and educated, a number of cooking shows began featuring local and regional restaurant chefs preparing signature dishes. At the same time many chefs were becoming local, and even national, celebrities. Series such as *The Great Chefs Of...* and *New York's Master Chefs* used new lightweight camera equipment to give the public a glimpse of what went on behind the scenes in these fabled kitchens.

Perhaps as an antidote to the number of white toques dominating the screen, an ordained Methodist minister who implored his viewers to "eat history" became TV's next cooking superstar. Jeff Smith, aka *The Frugal Gourmet* (now there's a name cash-strapped public television could love), was actually on the air in the '70s, but the show wasn't distributed nationally until later. By the mid-'80s and well into the '90s, he was the most-watched cook on PBS, and his show was beamed into 98 percent of American households. "Food, for me, is a classic device for discussing theology," he told *Newsweek* in 1987, and viewers ate up not just his simple recipes but his mini-histories on dish origins and his homilies on the sacrosanctity of breaking bread with family and friends.

Two other avowed non-chefs with weekday-dinner recipes for time-pressed home cooks emerged in the '80s. Nathalie Dupree, a Cordon Bleu (London)-trained chef who ran her own restaurant in an Atlanta suburb and founded Rich's Cooking School, introduced Dixie cooking to mainstream America with *New Southern Cooking* in 1986. Later shows like her 1998 series *Nathalie Dupree Entertains* downplayed the Southern focus, not because she was ashamed of her roots but she felt limited being pigeonholed as a Southern cook. "You can't take the South out of me, and I don't want to take the South out of me. I just think there ought to be a lot more South in the rest of the country," she told *USA Today* in 1998.

Food columnist Marcia Adams made it her mission to preserve and share what she calls the "attic receipts" of America's heartland ("recipes that are a bit out of fashion and are recorded in fading handwritten ledgers or tattered cards in Aunt Sarah's trunk," she writes in the introduction to the companion cookbook to her series *Amish Cooking from Quilt Country*). Thanks to her documentation and promotion, the traditional handicrafts and cooking of the Amish, Mennonites, Shakers, and others will endure for future generations to appreciate.

America also was growing more and more cholesterol-conscious, and the 1986 nutrition-centered cooking series by *New York Times* health columnist Jane Brody foreshadowed the fat-busting programs of Graham Kerr, Lynn Fischer, Jacques Pépin, and others that would come a few years hence.

Fast-forward to the 1990s. The public television cooking show, now a mature and prospering genre, has truly come of age. Studio kitchen productions now have shooting down to a science, with cameras mounted over the stove so viewers can peak into the pot to see the dumplings simmer just as well as the TV chef. Behind-the-scenes prep work has grown so sophisticated that for a segment on breadmaking for *Baking with Julia*, seventeen mixers were chugging at once in order for the dough to be shown at various stages, with several back-ups handy.

A bigger breakthrough, perhaps, is that technology has improved enough for the hand-held camera to break down the kitchen wall and take the TV talent on the road. Although hand-held cameras first captured Julia on a fishing boat, touring an artichoke farm, and on other foraging expeditions for *Dinner at Julia's* in 1983, the cost was too prohibitive for the practice to become widespread until later. The cooking-show-cum-travelogue (the Frug traipsing through bakeries in Bologna, Pierre Franey sailing over French vineyards in a hot air balloon, food journalist Burt Wolf traveling the globe for gastronomic adventures) hooked a new audience of vicarious travelers, who joined the food mavens in front of the tube.

After a ten-year hiatus from the small screen, Julia returned in 1993 with *Cooking with Master Chefs*, her first series produced with A La Carte Communications (who did *The Frugal Gourmet* in the '90s, among other series) and Maryland Public Television. She became what she (and *Sesame Street's* Cookie Monster) would call the "Alistair Cookie" of the cooking world, introducing the next generation of culinary all-stars instead of doing the chopping and dicing herself. (According to the Fitch biography, she had harbored this dream since her days as The French Chef.) She reprised her "Grande Dame of American Cooking" role for two later series, both of which turned the kitchen of her longtime Cambridge, Massachusetts, home into a de facto studio. *In Julia's Kitchen with Master Chefs* and *Baking with Julia* were the first cooking series to garner national Emmy awards.

In 1993, The Food Network, a cable TV channel devoted entirely to food programming, was born. Although cable channels like Lifetime, Discovery, and The Learning Channel ran some original programming, heretofore most of public TV's cooks found that their chief competition was, in fact, reruns of themselves— *The Frugal Gourmet*, *Yan Can Cook*, and other shows that lived on in cable perpetuity after public television's air rights expired. The new competition seemed to energize public television and the other cable networks, and a wonderful crossover of talents emerged, bringing to public television, to name just a few, Caprial Pence, Debbi Fields, and those marvelous British heavy-weight imports, Jennifer Paterson and Clarissa Dickson Wright (better known as the Two Fat Ladies).

Meanwhile, public television stations across the country began to recognize that cooking shows, which already fulfilled their basic mission to provide instructional programming, could do more. In an age where mass media are often accused of homogenizing the culture, what better way to preserve a region's unique identity than by exploring its culinary heritage? An explosion of regionally based cooking shows issued forth in the '90s. New Orleans public TV station WYES (which also produced Justin Wilson's shows) aired *Breakfast from New Orleans* (from the landmark Brennan's restaurant) as well as several series by famed chef Paul Prudhomme. "We're not going to do a show on chefs of the Great Northern Woods," quipped a station publicist in a 1995 interview with *Current*, a public broadcasting trade newspaper. (Louisiana's rich and varied cuisine is particularly well represented on public television; there's also the long-running *A Taste of Louisiana* with chef John Folse, produced by Louisiana Public Television.) To name just a representative handful, San Francisco's KQED presented *Weir Cooking in the Wine Country*, Maryland Public Television gave us *Chesapeake Bay Cooking with John Shields*, Arizona station KAET issued *Savor the Southwest* with Barbara Pool Fenzl, and Hawaii Public Television has produced several series with Hawaiian chef Roy Yamaguchi to publicize the islands' traditional and Pacific Rim cooking.

Ethnic cooking shows sprang up to fill our metaphysical hunger to learn about our roots as well as our very tangible hankering for authentic cuisine. Efrain Martinez ("Chef Ef") opened our eyes to the glories of Spanish cooking and Joan Nathan brought us the traditions and recipes of the Jewish kitchen. Shows like *Ciao Italia*, *Cucina Amore*, *Bugialli's Italy*, *The de'Medici Kitchen*, and *Lidia's Italian Table* helped make risotto and polenta as common as pasta and mashed potatoes on the dinner table.

The current proliferation of cooking shows also has given public TV license to explore specialized subjects that might have been rejected a decade earlier for not having mainstream appeal. To wit, we have George Hirsch's shows on grilling techniques, Molly Katzen's vegetarian recipes, and Jacques Torres' show-stopping desserts. Another emerging trend as the decade, century, and millenium draw to a close, is the appeal of tandem cooking teams, which include prolific virtuoso Jacques Pépin pairing first with daughter Claudine, and now with Julia; Annmarie Huste and John Mariani (*Crazy for Food*); and of course, the delightfully off-the-wall Fat Ladies.

Public television cooking shows can take some credit for an evolution, some might say revolution, in American taste and habits. Fine dining and serious cooking proliferate in restaurants, cooking schools, and more and more home kitchens. Although the genre continues to evolve, the public interest in cooking programs shows no signs of abating. What will the future of public television

cookery bring? Whatever it is, we will assuredly eat—and learn—well.

This volume is a commemorative collection of 100 mouth-watering recipes. It includes all-new dishes first seen live on *An American Feast*, plus a sampling of the best recipes previously published by America's favorite public television cooking stars. Each chapter is anchored by one of the five chefs featured in *An American Feast*, and includes the recipes prepared by that chef on the show. The chapters correspond to the stages of our feast: Starters, First Courses and Side Dishes, Main Courses—Fish and Seafood, Main Courses—Meat and Poultry, Desserts and Breads.

The recipes represent over two dozen cookbooks, published in many recipe styles. To celebrate the differences, they mostly have been left true to their original form, with only slight editing changes. Enjoy the feast and the variations you can create.

# *Starters*
## WITH MARTIN YAN

Martin Yan, America's foremost Chinese chef, has been wowing TV audiences with his lightning cleaver skills since 1982—making his *Yan Can Cook* series one of the longest-running hits on public television. His flashy knife work and natural showmanship on camera belie decades of serious culinary training that began when he escaped the poverty of his Guangzhou, China, home by working in his uncle's Hong Kong restaurant. After graduating from a cooking institute there, Martin journeyed west, at first living in Canada and eventually earning bachelor's and master's degrees in food science at the University of California at Davis. He opened the first Asian cooking school in Alberta, which led to a local cooking show. When the Canadian winters became too much, Martin returned to California, where his public television series quickly earned him a national following. His latest shows contain gorgeous footage of the restaurants, shops, and marketplaces of Asian cities Martin toured in search of recipes to share.

In the days before woks could be found at any department store, Martin not only introduced us to the glories of Asian cuisine but taught us not to be intimidated by it. His recipes for appetizers and other delicious nibbles capture his contagious zest for cooking and sharing food with friends.

# South Pacific Chicken Satay

Martin Yan                                                                    Serves 4

**Spice Paste**

2 stalks lemongrass

¼ cup water

4 walnut-size shallots

4 cloves garlic

1½ teaspoons fennel seed

1½ tablespoons packed brown sugar

1 tablespoon oyster-flavored sauce

2 teaspoons sesame oil

1½ teaspoons ground coriander

1½ teaspoons galangal powder (optional)

1½ teaspoons turmeric powder

1 teaspoon ground cumin

1 pound boneless, skinless chicken

20 bamboo skewers

Satay Peanut Sauce (recipe follows)

Lettuce leaves

Sliced cucumber, onion, and fresh chili

Thinly slice bottom 6 inches of lemongrass. Place in a blender with water, shallots, garlic, and fennel seed; process until smooth. Pour into a medium bowl. Add brown sugar, oyster-flavored sauce, sesame oil, coriander, galangal (if using), turmeric, and cumin; mix well.

Cut chicken into thin slices. Add chicken to spice paste and stir to coat. Cover and refrigerate for 2 hours or up to overnight.

Soak skewers in water for 15 minutes, or until ready to use.

Thread 2 pieces of chicken on each skewer. Place skewers on a preheated, oiled grill. Cook, turning skewers frequently, until chicken is cooked, 2 to 3 minutes.

Serve with satay peanut sauce for dipping, and garnish with lettuce leaves, cucumber, onion, and chili.

## Satay Peanut Sauce

Makes about 2 cups

**Spice Paste**

1 stalk lemongrass

¼ cup water

2 walnut-size shallots

2 cloves garlic

1 teaspoon ground coriander

1 teaspoon galangal powder (optional)

½ teaspoon ground cumin

1¼ cups roasted peanuts

3 tablespoons cooking oil

1 cup water

¼ cup packed brown sugar

3 tablespoons chili garlic sauce

2 tablespoons soy sauce

Thinly slice bottom 6 inches of lemongrass. Place in a blender with remaining spice paste ingredients and process until smooth.

In a blender, process peanuts until finely chopped.

Place a wok over medium-low heat until hot. Add oil, swirling to coat sides. Add spice paste and cook, stirring, until fragrant, 6 to 8 minutes.

Add water, peanuts, brown sugar, chili garlic sauce, and soy sauce; stir until evenly blended. Bring to a boil. Reduce heat and simmer, stirring frequently, until sauce is slightly thickened, 4 to 5 minutes.

Serve with satay, for dipping.

# Lemony Cilantro Chicken Drumettes

Nathalie Dupree

**Drumettes, the top joint of the wing, are like miniature drumsticks. They may be purchased pre-cut, or the whole wing may be separated at the joints. Pre-cut ones may be smaller than the ones you would cut yourself. I use the wing tips for family snacks or in stock. The second (middle) portion has 2 bones. It is tasty, but I don't use it if people are eating off napkins, because it is more difficult to handle. I do use it for family. Drumettes require an abundance of paper napkins next to the place they are set out, as they are the ultimate finger-licking food. Saffron adds wonderful flavor, but if you are watching pennies or using saffron in another item in the menu, use turmeric instead, because this recipe can be expensive. Cilantro is also called Chinese parsley or fresh coriander and is very strong in flavor. For subtlety, use the lesser amount. If you love it, as I do, go the whole route!**

8 pounds chicken drumettes

1 teaspoon safffron threads or turmeric

¼ cup lemon juice

¼ cup boiling water

¼ cup grated fresh ginger

1 cup water

3 tablespoons vegetable oil

10 garlic cloves, finely chopped

2 to 6 cups (2 to 6 bunches) very finely chopped cilantro

1 or 2 fresh, hot green chile peppers, very finely chopped

4 teaspoons ground cumin

2 teaspoons ground coriander seeds

1 to 2 teaspoons salt, or to taste

**Garnish (optional)**

Cilantro sprigs

Lemon wedges

Preheat the oven to 500°F. Line two 9x13-inch baking and freezing pans with aluminum foil.

Cut wings into drumettes if necessary and arrange on the foil, trying not to overlap. Lay the wing on a clean surface, skin side down, and sever at each of the joints with a knife. In addition to the drumettes, you may use the portion with two bones as well, although its meat is not as accessible, or you may save them for another time. Save the tips for stock.

Place baking pans on the top rack of the oven until brown, about 5 minutes. Turn the drumettes over and return to the oven to brown, another 3 minutes. When both sides have browned, transfer the drumettes to paper towels and set aside, saving the pans.

Stir the saffron and lemon juice into the boiling water. Combine this mixture with the ginger and 1 cup water in a blender or food processor and purée to a smooth consistency.

In a heavy 10-inch skillet, heat the oil over medium-high heat. Add the garlic and cook until softened, about 2 minutes. Turn down the heat and stir in the cilantro, green chile, cumin, coriander, and salt. Add the saffron mixture to the pan and stir to mix. Turn up the heat, bring to the boil, and reduce the liquid until the sauce is thick, like salsa.

To serve now, arrange the drumettes on a serving platter and top with the warm sauce.

To make ahead, reline the two 9x13-inch baking/freezing pans with clean heavy-duty freezer aluminum foil. Arrange the drumettes in the pans and pour the sauce over the wings. Let cool. Wrap with heavy foil and label. Freeze flat in the pan rather than bunched in a plastic container. Remove the pan when frozen. If you are short of freezer space, use plastic freezer bags for storage.

Defrost the drumettes 36 hours in the refrigerator or remove from the foil and defrost in the microwave.

Thirty minutes before serving, preheat the broiler to 500°F. Drain the sauce into a microwave-safe container or saucepan. Bring to the boil, reduce the heat, and keep warm.

Run the drumettes on the foil under the broiler, being careful not to burn them, until crisped, about 5 minutes. Turn them over and crisp them on the other side. Arrange the drumettes on a serving platter, top with the reheated sauce, and garnish with sprigs of cilantro or lemon wedges, if desired.

*Tips: Do not peel ginger unless the skin is very thick and tough if you chop it in the food processor.*

*One bunch of cilantro from my grocery store, removed from stems, is about 1 cup chopped.*

*To chop large quantities of herbs, wash them, dry thoroughly on paper towels, spread out to air dry half an hour, and chop, being careful not to over chop, by hand or in the food processor. The rule is if you can tell what it is, it's not chopped finely enough!*

# Chicken Spring Roll
# with Cucumber Mango Relish

Roy Yamaguchi                                Makes 10 spring rolls

**Available in Asian markets, rice paper is a thin, round sheet made of ground rice and salt. Use the standard 8-inch size in the following recipe.**

### Chicken Mixture

- ½ teaspoon minced ginger
- ¼ teaspoon minced basil
- ½ teaspoon minced garlic
- 1 teaspoon minced lemongrass
- ¼ cup chopped green onion
- 2 tablespoons olive oil
- ¼ cup dried shiitake mushrooms
- ¼ cup dried water chestnuts
- ¼ cup bean thread noodles, boiled, strained and coarsely chopped
- ¼ cup finely chopped mustard cabbage (Chinese cabbage) or Napa cabbage
- 1½ teaspoons fish sauce
- 1 pound raw chicken, coarsely chopped

### Spring Rolls

- 1 teaspoon sugar
- 1 cup hot water
- 10 (8-inch) rice paper wrappers
- 1 quart frying oil

### Relish

- 1 tablespoon minced ginger
- ¼ teaspoon minced garlic
- 2 tablespoons olive oil
- ½ teaspoon spicy sesame oil
- ½ cup seedless cucumber, diced, skin on
- ½ cup tomatoes, diced
- ½ cup mango, diced
- ¼ teaspoon soy sauce
- 1 teaspoon Lingham chili sauce, or any spicy/sweet sauce

### Preparation of the chicken mixture

In a skillet, brown the ginger, basil, garlic, lemongrass and green onion in the oil over high heat for 10 seconds.

Add the mushrooms, water chestnuts, noodles and mustard cabbage and sauté for 1 minute.

Season the mixture with the fish sauce, and place it in a large bowl. Once it has cooled, add the chicken and mix all ingredients well.

Season the mixture with more fish sauce or salt and pepper if needed.

### Preparation of the spring rolls

Dissolve the sugar in the hot water. Dip each rice paper wrapper in the sugar water until it is flexible.

Place ½ cup of the chicken mixture near the bottom edge of each piece of rice paper. Fold both edges in and continue to roll.

Deep-fry the rolls in the oil at 375 degrees for 15 minutes, or until they turn golden brown.

### Preparation of the relish

Sauté the ginger and garlic in the olive oil and sesame oil in a small pan over medium heat for about 10 seconds.

Quickly add the cucumber, tomato and mango. Toss the mixture for 10 seconds.

Remove the mixture from the heat and season it with soy sauce and chili sauce.

### Assembly

Cut the spring rolls in half. Place the slices on the plate, cut side down, and garnish with the relish.

# Lobster Potstickers

Martin Yan                                    Makes 30 dumplings

## Dipping Sauce

- ⅓ cup rice vinegar
- 2 tablespoons soy sauce
- 1 tablespoon chili garlic sauce
- 2 teaspoons black bean garlic sauce
- 1 teaspoon sesame oil

## Filling

- 8 ounces lobster meat, coarsely chopped
- ¼ cup finely chopped bamboo shoots
- 1 egg white
- 1 tablespoon shredded basil
- 1 tablespoon cornstarch
- 1 tablespoon dry sherry
- 2 teaspoons finely minced ginger
- 2 teaspoons sesame oil
- ¼ teaspoon salt
- ¼ teaspoon white pepper

- 30 potsticker wrappers
- 3 tablespoons cooking oil
- ⅔ cup water
- Basil sprigs, for garnish

Combine the dipping sauce ingredients in a small bowl; set aside.

Combine filling ingredients in a medium bowl; mix well. To shape each potsticker, place 1 heaping teaspoon of filling in center of a potsticker wrapper. Brush edges of wrapper with water, fold wrapper in half, crimping one side, to form a semicircle. Pinch edges together to seal. Cover potstickers with a dry towel to prevent drying.

Place a wide frying pan over medium heat until hot. Add 1½ tablespoons of the cooking oil, swirling to coat sides. Stand potstickers, half at a time, seam side up. Cook until bottoms are golden brown, 2 to 3 minutes. Add ⅓ cup of the water; reduce heat to low, cover, and cook until liquid is absorbed, 3 to 4 minutes. Uncover the skillet and cook an additional 1 to 2 minutes to recrisp the bottoms of the potstickers. Place potstickers on a serving plate; keep warm. Cook remaining potstickers with remaining oil and water.

Garnish potstickers with basil. Serve with dipping sauce.

# Mussels with Tomato, Celery and Saffron Butter

Rick Stein                                                    Serves 4 to 6

**This recipe uses mussel shells as a natural container for serving at a drinks party, without need of knives, forks or plates. The mussels are served on the half shell with a rich saffron butter sauce, some finely chopped celery that has been lightly cooked so it is still a little crunchy, and some finely diced good, sweet tomatoes.**

2 pounds mussels, cleaned

4 tablespoons dry white wine

2½ cups fish stock

¼ teaspoon saffron threads

3 ounces inner stalks of celery, finely diced (about ⅔ cup)

3 tomatoes, peeled, seeded and finely diced

¾ cup chilled unsalted butter, cut into small pieces

Juice of ¼ lemon

Salt and freshly ground black pepper

Put the mussels into a large pan with 1 tablespoon of the wine. Cover and cook over high heat for about 3 to 4 minutes, shaking the pan every now and then, until the mussels have opened. Discard any that remain closed. Remove from the heat, strain off the juice and stir 2 tablespoons of it into the stock. Discard the remainder.

Bring the stock, the remaining wine and the saffron to a boil and boil rapidly until reduced to about 4 tablespoons.

Meanwhile, bring a small pan of salted water to a boil, add the celery and cook for 1 minute. Drain and refresh under cold running water, then set aside.

Preheat the oven to 275°F.

Remove the top half of each mussel shell, leaving the mussel in the other half. Lay them side by side in a shallow ovenproof serving dish. Put the diced celery and tomato on top of the mussels and season with a little salt and black pepper. You can do

this up to an hour beforehand if you wish, but don't refrigerate the cooked mussels as they never taste the same again. Cover with plastic wrap, however, to stop them drying out.

When you are ready to serve, remove the plastic wrap and cover the mussels with aluminum foil. Warm through in the oven for just a few minutes. Meanwhile, bring the reduced stock back to a boil and then whisk in the butter a few pieces at a time, adding more as the butter amalgamates. I prefer to make these mounted butter sauces over a brisk heat, adding the butter and whisking all the time. The action of boiling stock with the butter causes a natural liaison. If the sauce separates, simply add a little more water, bring it back to a boil and it will cohere again. Stir in the lemon juice and season with salt and pepper to taste. Remove the mussels from the oven, uncover, and spoon a little of the sauce over each one. Serve immediately.

# Grilled Littlenecks on the Half-Shell

Madeleine Kamman                                    Serves 4 to 6

**My favorite clam on the half-shell is the littleneck clam.**

36 littleneck clams

2 tablespoons finely diced ginger, blanched in boiling water

2 tablespoons finely chopped scallion greens

Salt

Pepper from the mill

1 tablespoon Worcestershire sauce

½ cup butter

⅓ cup heavy cream

Kosher or coarse salt as needed

Open the littlenecks, making sure that you pass your knife blade under each clam to sever its muscle and make the clam easy to remove from the shell at the table.

Put the ginger, scallion greens, salt and pepper to your taste, Worcestershire sauce and butter in a food processor. Cream together well and gradually add the heavy cream.

Correct the seasoning. Put a small teaspoon of the mixture on top of each raw clam.

Sprinkle a ¼-inch-thick layer of kosher salt onto a large jelly-roll pan, set the clams on it and broil them for a few minutes, or until golden. Serve piping hot with crusty bread.

# Tonnato Dip

Lynn Fischer                                    Makes 2¼ cups

**This makes a delicious spread for toasted baguettes or any flat bread. It is also an excellent filling for hard-cooked egg whites. To serve as a dip with vegetables, stir in 1/4 cup nonfat sour cream.**

1 clove garlic, chopped

2 tablespoons fresh lemon juice

1 teaspoon anchovy paste

2 tablespoons egg substitute

3 tablespoons capers plus 2 teaspoons caper liquid

½ teaspoon Worcestershire

1 6-ounce can tuna packed in water, undrained, or 6 ounces fresh

Freshly ground black pepper

1 large slice fresh white bread, torn into pieces

2 tablespoons olive oil

¼ cup fresh chopped parsley

In a food processor or blender, puree garlic, lemon juice, anchovy paste, egg substitute, 1 tablespoon capers and caper liquid, Worcestershire, tuna and its liquid, pepper, and bread. With the motor running, drizzle in the olive oil. Remove to a serving bowl, cover, and refrigerate until chilled. Garnish with remaining capers and parsley, surrounded with fresh vegetables and crackers.

# Hummus Bi Tahini

Nick Stellino

Serves 4 to 6

**Chickpeas are used throughout the Mediterranean, but perhaps nowhere with such universal appeal as in this traditional Lebanese spread. For the ultimate rendition, make pita bread from scratch; then sit back, and savor.**

- 1 (15-ounce) can chickpeas (garbanzos), drained
- 4 tablespoons lemon juice
- 4 tablespoons roasted tahini (sesame seed paste)
- 2 tablespoons hot water
- ½ teaspoon salt
- 2 garlic cloves
- ⅛ teaspoon ground cumin
- ⅛ teaspoon cayenne pepper
- 1 tablespoon extra virgin olive oil
- ⅛ teaspoon paprika
- 1 tablespoon chopped fresh Italian parsley
- Pita bread, cut into wedges

Place the chickpeas, lemon juice, tahini, water, salt, garlic, cumin and cayenne pepper in the bowl of a food processor or blender. Process for 1½–2 minutes, until smooth.

If serving immediately, spoon the hummus into a serving bowl, drizzle with the olive oil and sprinkle with the paprika and parsley. Serve with the wedges of pita bread for dipping.

If the hummus is being prepared ahead of time, cover the bowl and refrigerate for up to 1 week. (The intensity of the garlic will increase as the hummus ages.)

*Wine Suggestion: Gewürztraminer*

# Cheese Balls Stuffed with Olives
## *Relleno de Aceitunas (Bolitas)*

Efrain Martinez, Chef Ef

Serves 4

**This is really fun food. The *bolitas* are fun to make, fun to serve, and definitely fun to eat. From the crispy crust to the sweet pimento stuffing, this delightful dish will surely please everyone.**

- 1 cup shredded sharp cheddar cheese
- ¼ teaspoon paprika
- 2 teaspoons butter
- ½ cup flour
- 25 stuffed small olives, rinsed and drained

In a food processor or blender, mix all the ingredients except the olives and blend until smooth.

Place one teaspoon of the mixture over each olive and shape it into a ball by rolling it with the palm of your hand. Repeat the process until all the olives have been rolled.

Place the olives in a greased or oiled baking pan and bake in a 400°F preheated oven for about 15 minutes.

Remove to a serving platter and serve at room temperature.

# Country Pâté
## *Pâté de Campagne*

Julia Child

**This is an especially easy pâté to make—grind everything together, pack neatly in a buttered loaf pan, and it's ready for the oven. Make it more elaborate if you wish, since pâtés are built according to cook's mood-of-the-day. Layer strips of ham or chicken as you pack in the meat, for instance—a quarter pound would do. Or you might fold peeled pistachios into the mixture. Such touches as these make it your very own.**

⅔ cup minced onions cooked until translucent in 2 table-spoons butter

1¼ pounds (2½ cups) pork sausage meat, your own or store-bought

¾ pound (1½ cups) raw chicken breasts

½ pound (1 cup) pork or beef liver

1 cup lightly pressed down crumbs made from fresh homemade type white bread

1 large egg

⅓ cup cream cheese or goat cheese

1 medium clove of garlic, puréed

2 to 3 tablespoons good brandy

1 tablespoon salt

¼ teaspoon each ground allspice and thyme

¼ teaspoon ground imported bay leaf

¼ teaspoon freshly ground pepper

### The mixture

Purée all the ingredients together in a food processor; or put them through the fine blade of a meat grinder, then beat in a large mixing bowl to blend. To check seasoning, sauté a spoonful in a small frying pan, let cool, and taste it analytically; correct as necessary, exaggerating the flavors since pâtés are served cold.

### Assembling and baking

Pack into a well-buttered loaf pan, cover with buttered wax paper, then with foil, allowing only 1 inch of overhang. Bake in a bain-marie (a pan of boiling water) in a 350°F oven. It is done in 1¼ to 1½ hours at a meat thermometer reading of 162°F—when the meat is pressed, the juices are pale yellow with just a trace of rosy color.

### Cooling

When done, let cool for an hour, then weight down with a twin pan or a board and a 5-pound weight (such as a canned good). When cool, cover and refrigerate—let the pâté mellow for a day or two before serving.

### Serving

Set the baking dish over heat for a few seconds to loosen the pâté; pour out fat and juices, and unmold the pâté onto a platter. Scrape and wipe off the surface. Decorate the top with parsley, pimiento strips, or whatever seems appropriate.

# Cheese-Nut Pâté

Mollie Katzen                                    Serves 8 to 10 as an appetizer

I think I've made this pâté more than any other recipe in my book. It is especially easy if you use a food processor, first to grate the cheddar, and then to purée everything together. You can get truly artful with the decorations. The pâté gets frosted all over with ricotta cheese, and then embellished ad infinitum with vegetable slices, minced herbs, nuts, olives, etc. The dish creates a festive event in and of itself, and your guests will feel flattered. The pâté can be assembled and baked up to four days ahead. Wrap it airtight and store in the refrigerator. Frost and garnish within hours of serving.

2 tablespoons melted butter (to grease the pan)

1 cup finely minced onion

1 tablespoon butter

8 ounces cream cheese (lowfat okay)

1 pound cottage cheese (lowfat okay)

1 cup ground almonds and walnuts, combined (use a food processor with steel blade or a blender, in quick spurts)

½ teaspoon salt (or to taste)

Lots of black pepper

1 tablespoon minced fresh dill (or 1 teaspoon dried)

2 teaspoons prepared mustard

2 to 3 teaspoons fresh lime or lemon juice

2 cups (packed) grated cheddar

**Toppings:**

1 cup ricotta

A few walnut halves, whole almonds, and whole or chopped olives

Radishes, cucumber slices, and parsley

Preheat oven to 325°. Melt and distribute 2 tablespoons butter in a standard loaf pan.

In a small pan, sauté onions in 1 tablespoon butter until soft.

Combine and whip together all ingredients (except those for topping). Use the steel blade attachment on a food processor, or high speed on an electric mixer.

When mixture is uniform, spread evenly into greased loaf pan.

Bake 1 hour. (When you take it out of the oven it will look suspiciously loose, but don't worry. It firms up as it chills.) Allow to cool completely in the pan, then chill for at least several hours before turning out onto a serving platter.

To get the pâté out of the pan, loosen it with a spatula. Invert it onto a larger plate, holding the pan in place against the plate. Shake firmly several times (or give it a whack). Remove the loaf pan. The pâté should emerge in one piece. If it breaks, you can easily mold it back together. (Don't be discouraged by how ugly it looks in its predecorated state. It will be transformed by the ricotta and the garnishes.)

To decorate, spread a layer of ricotta cheese all over, as if frosting a cake. Place whole or half nuts, olives, radishes, cucumber slices, and parsley in the design of your choice. Serve with dark bread or good crackers.

# Beef Nachos

Barbara Pool Fenzl                                          Makes about 40 nachos

**In the Southwest, nachos range from a snack topped with just cheese and chiles to a more substantial appetizer like this one. Pickled jalapeños are found in the condiment section of most grocery stores. They're quite hot, but they add just the right amount of pizzazz to the meat mixture. The pungency of commercial chile powders can vary from brand to brand, so find one whose heat suits your palate.**

½ pound lean ground chuck

1 tablespoon freshly squeezed lime juice

2 tablespoons finely chopped red onion

1 tablespoon finely chopped pickled jalapeño chiles

¼ teaspoon salt

¼ teaspoon chile powder

¼ cup finely chopped cilantro

1 cup grated queso fresco, cotija, or Monterey jack cheese

40 tortilla chips

½ cup sour cream, for garnish

40 fresh cilantro leaves, for garnish

Preheat a broiler.

In a bowl, stir together the beef, lime juice, onion, jalapeños, salt, chile powder, cilantro, and cheese. Gently spread each tortilla chip with a thin layer of the mixture (about 1 tablespoon per chip). Place on a baking sheet and broil 6 inches from the heat until the meat is completely cooked and the cheese is melted, 3 to 4 minutes.

Top each nacho with a dollop of sour cream and a cilantro leaf. Place the finished nachos on a serving platter and serve immediately.

*Do Ahead: The nacho mixture can be made up to 4 hours ahead of time, covered, and refrigerated. Bring to room temperature before spreading on tortilla chips.*

# Steamed Pork Siu Mai

Martin Yan                                                    Makes 30 siu mai

**Filling**

½ pound ground pork

2 ounces medium-size raw shrimp, shelled and deveined

1 Chinese sausage or 2 slices lean smoked bacon, coarsely chopped

1½ tablespoons cornstarch

2 teaspoons dry sherry

1 tablespoon oyster-flavored sauce

1 teaspoon chopped mint leaves

1 teaspoon sesame oil

**Dipping Sauce**

¼ cup soy sauce

1 tablespoon hot mustard powder

30 siu mai or wonton wrappers

¼ cup frozen green peas, thawed

In a food processor, process filling ingredients into a paste. Transfer to a stainless steel bowl. Combine dipping sauce in a small bowl; blend well.

To fill each dumpling, spoon 1 heaping teaspoon of filling into center of each wrapper, keeping remaining wrappers covered to prevent drying. Use fingers to form an open-topped pouch.

Place one green pea on top of each siu mai; place siu mai on two greased 9-inch pie pans or other heatproof dish.

Place a steaming rack in a wok. Add water and bring to a boil. Place dish on the rack cover and steam over medium-high heat for 20 minutes. Check the water level in the wok occasionally. If it is low, add boiling water to avoid lowering the temperature. When the siu mai are cooked, remove the dish from the wok. Serve the first portion while cooking the remain siu mai. Serve siu mai with dipping sauce.

# Herbed Spiced Nuts

Burt Wolf                                                      Makes 3 cups

1 cup macadamia or hazelnuts

1 cup shelled pistachios

1 cup raw cashews

1 tablespoon unsalted butter

1 clove garlic, crushed

1 teaspoon dried rosemary, crushed

½ teaspoon dried thyme, crushed

¼ teaspoon cayenne or less to taste

¾ teaspoon kosher salt

Preheat the oven to 350°F. Spread the nuts on a roasting pan and toast in the oven until they are golden brown, about 10 minutes. While the nuts are toasting, heat the butter in a pan with the crushed garlic, herbs, and cayenne.

Remove the garlic from the butter and discard. Toss the toasted nuts in a bowl with the flavored butter and the salt. Cool and serve.

# Warm Olives with Fennel and Orange

Joanne Weir                                                                 Serves 6

**A glass of chilled champagne and a plate of warm olives studded with orange, fennel, and garlic is a perfect way to start any evening in the wine country. The briny, slightly salty flavor of the olives pairs well with a yeasty champagne or sparkling wine. Any leftovers? Place them in a Mason jar and store them in the refrigerator for up to a month. To serve, simply warm them gently.**

2 oranges

Salt

1 medium fennel bulb, cut into eighths

¾ cup extra-virgin olive oil

½ teaspoon fennel seed, coarsely cracked

4 garlic cloves, peeled and thinly sliced

⅛ teaspoon crushed red pepper flakes

4 ounces Niçoise olives

4 ounces green picholine olives

2 ounces oil-cured olives

2 ounces Kalamata black olives

With a vegetable peeler, remove 8 strips of orange peel, each 2-inches long. Try not to remove any of the white pith. If there is white pith, scrape it off with a paring knife.

Bring a large pot of salted water to a boil. Add the fresh fennel and cook for 3 minutes. Remove from the heat and drain.

Warm the olive oil in a large saucepan. Add the orange peel, fresh fennel, fennel seed, garlic, and red pepper flakes and cook until they begin to sizzle, about 1 minute. Add the olives and warm gently for 5 minutes. Remove from the heat and let sit 6 hours. Discard the orange peel.

Ten minutes before serving, warm the olives again. To serve, place the olives and fennel on a small platter. Drizzle with a few tablespoons of the oil and serve immediately.

# Pansanella

John D. Folse                                                               Serves 4

3 cups diced Creole tomatoes

2 tablespoons chopped fresh basil

1 teaspoon chopped fresh thyme

½ cup extra virgin olive oil

¼ cup red wine vinegar

¾ cup grated Parmesan cheese

25 whole basil leaves

25 French bread croutons, toasted

Salt and black pepper

In a large mixing bowl, combine all ingredients except whole basil leaves and croutons. Blend well, cover and refrigerate 1–2 hours. When ready to serve, place one whole basil leaf on top of a French bread crouton and serve one heaping tablespoon of the Pansanella on top. Eat as a cold hors d'oeuvre.

# Pico de Gallo

Stephan Pyles

Literally meaning the "beak of a rooster," this simple but ubiquitous relish probably got its name in Mexico from the way it was eaten, with thumb and forefinger, mimicking the pecking action of a rooster. Pico do gallo varies from state to state in Mexico, even incorporating such diverse ingredients as jicama, orange, and pineapple. In Texas, however, this recipe is the "real deal."

5 medium-size ripe tomatoes, seeded and diced into ¼-inch pieces

1 tablespoon chopped fresh cilantro

1 garlic clove, minced

½ cup minced onion

Juice of ½ lime

2 serranos, seeded and minced

Salt to taste

Combine all the ingredients in a medium bowl. Let stand for at least 30 minutes. Serve chilled or at room temperature.

# Primo Guacamole

Stephan Pyles

Avocados, like tomatoes, are fruits. They are high in carotene, protein, and vitamins E and C—and their fat content is actually lower than most people think. Better yet, this native Mexican fruit has long had a reputation as an aphrodisiac. For best results, choose ripe, unblemished avocados and those that give gently when pressed.

¼ cup finely diced onion

2 garlic cloves, minced

2 serranos, seeded and diced

1 teaspoon chopped fresh cilantro

Juice of 1 lime

½ teaspoon salt

2 large very ripe avocados, peeled, pitted, and chopped

1 large ripe tomato, blanched, peeled, seeded, and diced

Combine the onion, garlic, serranos, cilantro, lime juice, and salt in a molcajete or mortar and pestle. Using the pestle of the molcajete, pulverize the mixture in the base. Add the avocados and tomato and continue to mash until thoroughly combined. Serve immediately.

# Onion Fritters

Marcia Adams

Makes 2 dozen fritters

**Some Amish and Mennonite cooks call these onion patties; call them what you will, they are a very special vegetable treat—crispy like an onion ring and full of flavor. Though devised to be part of a meal, I can recommend them as a cocktail accompaniment as well. Make a double recipe; these evaporate into thin air as soon as they appear.**

**Allow enough cooking oil so the fritters can cook without crowding. My deep-fryer uses three (24-ounce) bottles of peanut oil. An electric skillet or sauté pan can be used, which will require less oil.**

Peanut oil, for deep-frying
¾ cup all-purpose flour
1 tablespoon yellow cornmeal
1 tablespoon sugar
2 teaspoons baking powder
½ teaspoon salt
¼ teaspoon black pepper
Dash of grated nutmeg
½ cup cold milk
Dash of hot red pepper sauce
2½ cups finely chopped onions

Heat the peanut oil to 375°F. in a deep-fryer or deep, straight-sided pan. Meanwhile, in a large mixing bowl, whisk together the flour, cornmeal, sugar, baking powder, salt, pepper, and nutmeg. Stir in the milk to make a thick batter, smoothing out the lumps. Add the pepper sauce and onions; mix well.

Drop several heaping teaspoonfuls of batter into the hot oil and begin turning the first fritter over as soon as you finish dropping in the last teaspoonful of batter. Fry until golden brown on both sides, then remove with slotted spoon to a paper towel to drain. Serve immediately! And you won't regret the double recipe!

# Old-Fashioned Spicy Lemonade

Marcia Adams

Makes a scant quart syrup; approximately 32 glasses

**Lemonade is a favorite beverage in Amish and Mennonite communities, not just in the summer but year-round. Lemons were at one time considered a great luxury and if a housewife had six lemons a year, she considered herself very lucky. When refrigeration was not available, lemons were stored, buried in sand, in crocks. This version starts with a spicy lemon syrup base that can be kept on hand in the refrigerator; it is very convenient and most refreshing after a hot summer day of antiquing.**

3 tablespoons lemon zest
4 cups sugar
4 cups water
2 cinnamon sticks
Juice of 6 lemons, strained
Additional lemon slices studded with whole cloves, or fresh mint

In a deep saucepan, combine the lemon zest, sugar, water, and cinnamon sticks. Bring the mixture to a rolling boil. Boil gently, uncovered, over medium heat for 5 minutes. Remove from the heat and cool. Strain the mixture through a fine wire sieve or cheesecloth. Add the strained lemon juice to the sugar syrup. Transfer to a glass container and refrigerate until needed.

To make the lemonade, mix 4 tablespoons of the lemon syrup with 1 cup of cold water. Fill 2 water glasses with ice and pour in the lemonade; this is enough for 2 average-size water glasses. Garnish and serve.

# Tropical Margarita

Stephan Pyles                    Makes 4 cocktails

**This margarita takes me back to the Yucatan peninsula where I was inspired to develop it. Bananas and passion fruit are an incredible combination in any case, and their flavors accentuate the sweet-sour components of the classic margarita.**

½ cup fresh lime juice
  (4 to 6 limes)
5 tablespoons superfine sugar
1 very ripe banana
¼ cup passion fruit purée
¾ cup good-quality tequila
  (4 jiggers)
1½ ounces Triple Sec (1 jigger)
  Crushed ice

Combine the lime juice and sugar in a large bowl. Let stand, stirring occasionally, until the sugar dissolves completely. Purée the banana with the passion fruit purée in a blender; add the tequila and Triple Sec and blend until smooth, about 30 seconds. Serve in margarita glasses over crushed ice.

# Watermelon Margarita

Stephan Pyles                    Makes 4 cocktails

**This margarita is the essence of peak summer flavor. The watermelon juice perfectly balances the lime, and the color from the melon makes a striking presentation.**

½ cup fresh lime juice
  (4 to 6 limes)
5 tablespoons superfine sugar
1 cup watermelon juice
  (made from puréed, strained
  watermelon)
¾ cup good-quality tequila
  (4 jiggers)
1½ ounces Triple Sec (1 jigger)
  Crushed ice

Combine the lime juice and sugar in a large bowl. Let stand, stirring occasionally, until the sugar dissolves completely. Add the watermelon juice, tequila and Triple Sec to the lime juice mixture; combine thoroughly. Serve in margarita glasses over crushed ice.

# First Courses and Side Dishes

## WITH LIDIA MATTICCHIO BASTIANICH

Lidia Matticchio Bastianich was born in a small town in Istria, a peninsula on the Adriatic "where food was the center of life," she writes in her first cookbook, *La Cucina di Lidia*. In the hardscrabble landscape of post-war Europe her family made the most of little.

Lidia learned how to stretch a scrawny chicken into a three-course feast, collect clams from the seashore, forage mushrooms from the forest, and harvest olives from her grandparents' groves. This intimate connection to the cycles and seasons of food preparation was valuable training for the future restaurateur.

Italy ceded Istria to Yugoslavia after World War II, and Lidia's family immigrated to America when she was twelve. When she married Felice Bastianich, they shared a dream of opening a resaurant. After two successful ventures in Queens, N.Y., they launched Felidia in Manhattan in 1981. It soon became one of the premier Italian restaurants in the country.

With a poet's passion and a food scholar's understanding, Lidia explains in her public television series *Lidia's Italian Table* (and in the companion cookbook of the same name) how home cooks can coax unimaginable intensity of flavor from pastas, soups, salads, and other first course offerings by combining a reverence for fresh ingredients with careful cooking, judicious seasoning, and an unhurried attitude.

# Risotto with Wild Mushrooms and Truffles
## *Risotto al Funghi e Tartufo*

Lidia Matticchio Bastianich                                      Serves 6

---

**For the Mushrooms**

¼ cup dry porcini mushrooms

½ cup strong hot chicken stock

12 ounces wild mushrooms (porcini, shiitakes, chanterelles, etc.)

2 tablespoons olive oil

½ teaspoon salt

**For the Rice**

3 tablespoons olive oil

1 cup minced onions

2 tablespoons minced shallots

2 cups Arborio rice

1 cup dry white wine

About 6 cups strong hot chicken stock

Salt

**For Serving**

2 to 4 tablespoons butter, cut into pieces

1 cup freshly grated, best quality Parmesan cheese

Freshly ground pepper

2 ounces white Alba truffle (optional)

**Preparing the mushrooms**

Rinse the dry porcini mushrooms, then soak in a bowl with the ½ cup hot chicken stock and set aside for 20 minutes. Trim the fresh wild mushrooms, discarding tough woody areas and damaged portions. (If necessary, wash briefly and dry in a towel.) Cut into ⅛-inch, lengthwise slices. Film the frying pan with olive oil. When hot, toss in the wild mushrooms, season with the salt, and sauté 5 minutes or more to evaporate moisture and to intensify their flavor.

**Preparing the risotto**

Meanwhile, heat the 3 tablespoons of oil in the sauté pan and add the onions. Sauté, stirring frequently, until translucent, then add the shallots and sauté for a moment more. Finally, stir in the rice, and "toast it" by stirring rather slowly and fairly constantly over moderately high heat until the grains begin to turn golden, and to feel loose and dry—they will click softly in the pan. At once, add the wine; turn the heat fairly high to boil it down. When the rice is almost dry, ladle in enough hot stock barely to cover it. Regulate heat so that stock just simmers, season with a little salt, and prepare to be near it and to stir it slowly and almost constantly from now on.

**Adding the mushrooms**

Continue to add stock as the rice absorbs it, and after the rice has cooked for about 8 minutes, stir in the sautéed wild mushrooms. Ladle ½ cup of stock into the sauté pan to deglaze it, and pour the liquid into the risotto. Remove the soaked porcini and squeeze their juices back into their bowl. Chop the porcini and stir into the risotto; then, being careful not to add any sand or sediment at the bottom of the bowl, pour the soaking juices into the risotto.

**Serving the risotto**

When the risotto is ready (the rice grains have doubled in size and are suspended in a creamy liquid, the rice should be just tender—al dente) remove it from heat, and immediately beat in the butter and half the cheese with a wooden spoon. Season with pepper to taste, serve immediately on a warm platter or warm soup plates. With a truffle shaver, shave the truffle (if using) all over each portion and serve immediately.

# Frittata with Aromatic Herbs
## *Frittata alle Erbe*

Giuliano Bugialli                                    Serves 6 to 8

**This frittata in its original version contains a festival of many wild greens, the exact combination being found only in that area, mountainous Friuli. We can approximate it with a gathering of greens and herbs available to us here: spinach, chard, leeks, sage, parsley, basil, marjoram, mint, and rosemary, all fresh if possible. The blending of so many herbs creates a wonderful freshness and combines into a convincing and original flavor.**

1½  pounds fresh spinach, large stems removed

1½  pounds fresh Swiss chard, large stems removed.

Coarse-grained salt

1  medium-size leek, white part only, or 1 yellow onion, cleaned

3  tablespoons (1½ ounces) sweet butter

3  tablespoons extra virgin olive oil

3  ounces pancetta, cut into small pieces or coarsely ground

1  large fresh sage leaf

5  sprigs fresh Italian parsley, leaves only

5  fresh basil leaves

1  tablespoon fresh marjoram leaves or large pinch of dried marjoram

10  fresh mint leaves

1  heaping teaspoon fresh rosemary leaves

Salt and freshly ground black pepper

5  extra-large eggs

**To Serve**

Fresh basil and Italian parsley leaves

Soak the spinach and Swiss chard in a large bowl of cold water for half an hour. Bring a large pot of cold water to a boil, add coarse salt to taste, then drain the vegetables, add them to the pot, and boil for 5 minutes.

Meanwhile rinse the leek very well and finely chop it on a cutting board.

Place a large casserole with the butter and 2 tablespoons of the olive oil over medium heat; when the butter is melted, add the leek and pancetta and sauté until the leek is translucent, 3 to 4 minutes. Finely chop the sage, parsley, basil, marjoram, mint, and rosemary together on a cutting board. Add them to the casserole and sauté for 5 minutes more.

Drain the cooked spinach and chard and cool them under cold running water. Lightly squeeze them and coarsely chop them on a cutting board. Add them to the casserole, mix very well, and season with salt and pepper. Cook for 10 minutes more, mixing every so often. Transfer the contents of the casserole to a crockery or glass bowl and let rest until cool, about half an hour.

Using a fork, lightly beat the eggs with salt and pepper to taste and pour them onto the cooled vegetables. Mix very well. Heat a 10-inch omelet pan with the remaining tablespoon olive oil over medium heat. When the pan is evenly hot, add the egg mixture. Level the mixture with a fork and keep puncturing the bottom with the fork as the eggs set, to allow the liquid on top to move through to the bottom. This will help the eggs to cook uniformly. When the eggs are well set and the frittata is well detached from the bottom of the pan, put a plate, upside down, over the pan and reverse the pan, turning the frittata out onto the plate. Return the pan to the heat and carefully slide the frittata into the pan and cook the other side. After 30 seconds, when the eggs should be well set, reverse the frittata onto a serving platter. Cut into wedges and serve warm or at room temperature after a few hours with the basil and parsley leaves.

# Spicy Capellini
## *Capellini Capricciosi*

Lidia Matticchio Bastianich                    Serves 4 to 6

---

8 slices of bacon, chopped

⅓ cup olive oil

2 medium onions, thinly sliced

8 Tuscan peperoncini, seeded and chopped (see note)

3 cups peeled Italian tomatoes, crushed

¼ teaspoon salt, or to taste

1 pound capellini

¾ cup grated Parmigiano Reggiano

In a non-reactive skillet, sauté the bacon in 3 tablespoons of olive oil until lightly browned. Add the onions and cook, stirring, over medium heat until golden. Add the peperoncini, crushed tomatoes, and salt and simmer for 10 minutes.

While the sauce is simmering, cook the capellini in 4 quarts of salted boiling water until *al dente* (tender but still firm), about 3 minutes. Drain the pasta and toss with the remaining olive oil. Stir in the sauce, add the cheese, toss well, and serve immediately. (This is the only exception in tossing pasta with olive oil before adding the sauce. The capellini are so thin that the coating of oil limits their absorption of the hot sauce and helps to keep them *al dente* for a longer period while eating them.)

*Note: Peperoncini (pickled hot Italian peppers) are available at specialty shops and most supermarkets.*

# Sardinian Artichoke Pie

Jennifer Paterson and Clarissa Dickson Wright, Two Fat Ladies

**Globe artichokes are very Elizabethan. They don't grow too well in Britain, so I snap them up whenever I see them. Out of season, they are good in jars, and any delicatessen worth its salt should have them. This makes a good vegetarian main course as well as an excellent supper dish. CDW**

28 artichoke hearts or 12 baby artichokes

1½ cups fresh white bread crumbs

2 cups grated Parmesan cheese

2 cups grated Romano cheese

3 tablespoons drained capers, chopped

½ pound ripe olives, pitted and halved

5 medium tomatoes, skinned and thinly sliced, or 1 large can plum tomatoes, drained and chopped

10 ounces Fontina or Gruyère cheese, thinly sliced

3 tablespoons olive oil

If using whole baby artichokes, trim the leaves, and boil the artichokes until tender. Drain and slice thinly.

Butter a 10-inch springform cake pan and coat with one-third of the bread crumbs. In a bowl, mix together the Parmesan, Romano, and the remaining bread crumbs. Arrange layers in the cake pan, beginning with the artichokes, followed by the capers and olives, tomatoes, Fontina, and then the bread crumb mixture. Drizzle 1 tablespoon of olive oil over this and repeat, pressing down well. These quantities should make three layers.

Bake in a preheated 350°F oven for 25 minutes. Leave to cool for 10 minutes, unmold, and serve with a salad.

# Three-Squash Soup with Orzo
## *Zuppa di Tre Zucche con Orzo*

Mary Ann Esposito                                    Makes 2½ quarts

**Orzo is better known as pearl barley and is a favorite addition to soups. It is just right in this glorious and hearty soup made with chunks of butternut and zucchini squash. Pureed spaghetti squash and cherry tomatoes are used to thicken the soup, giving it lots of flavor and texture. An added bonus is that the soup is very low in fat. Prepare the soup ingredients a day ahead by baking and pureeing the spaghetti squash, pureeing the tomatoes, and cutting up the vegetables.**

1¼ pounds spaghetti squash, cut in half, seeded, and cut into quarters

4½ cups water

1 tablespoon butter

1 pound leeks, white part only, washed well, cut in half lengthwise, and cut into ¼-inch-thick slices

2 zucchini (12 ounces total), cut in half lengthwise, then cut into ¼-inch-thick slices

1¼ pounds butternut squash, peeled, cut in half, seeded, and cut into ¼-inch pieces

4 cups pureed cherry tomatoes (2 pounds)

1 cup hot water

3½ teaspoons salt

¾ cup orzo or other small soup pasta

6 to 8 fresh basil leaves, minced

Preheat the oven to 375°F.

Place the spaghetti squash quarters cut side down in a baking pan with ½ cup of the water. Cover the pan with aluminum foil and bake until the squash is soft, about 30 minutes. When cool enough to handle, scoop the pulp from the cavity and transfer it to a food processor or blender. Puree the squash until smooth (you may have to do it in batches). There should be about 1½ cups. Transfer the squash to a bowl, cover, and refrigerate until ready to use. (Can be prepared a day or two ahead.)

While the squash is baking, melt the butter in a soup pot, add the leeks, and cook, covered, over low heat for 3 minutes, stirring a few times. Add the zucchini and butternut squash, stir to evenly mix the vegetables, cover the pot, and continue to cook over low heat for about 12 minutes. The vegetables should retain their shape and be *al dente* but cooked. Stir in the tomatoes, hot water, pureed squash, and 2 teaspoons of the salt. Cover and cook over low heat for 10 minutes.

Meanwhile, bring the remaining 4 cups water to a boil, stir in the remaining 1½ teaspoons salt and the orzo and cook until the orzo is *al dente*, about 10 minutes. Drain and stir the orzo into the soup. Stir in the basil and serve.

*Tip: Using a nonstick soup pot in this recipe eliminates the need to add much fat when cooking the leeks and vegetables.*

*Note: Spaghetti squash can be cooked in a microwave on high power for 5 to 6 minutes per pound. Be sure to pierce the rind first before microwaving to prevent an explosion.*

# Corn and Shrimp Chowder

Vertamae Grosvenor                                                    Serves 4 to 6

**If you like, omit the cream and add 1 large potato, cooked and mashed, with the stock. If the potato thickens the chowder too much, increase the stock to 3 cups.**

2 scallions

4 ears of corn

1 pound shrimp

3 tablespoons butter

2 cups chicken or fish stock

Salt and white pepper to taste

½ cup heavy cream

Thinly slice the scallions, including the tender green tops. Cut the kernels from the ears of corn; you should have about 2 cups. Peel the shrimp. Make a shallow incision along the back of each shrimp and lift out and discard the vein-like tract.

In a saucepan over medium heat, melt the butter. Add the scallions and sauté until softened, about 3 minutes. Pour in the stock and stir in the corn. Season with salt and white pepper and simmer, uncovered, for 10 minutes.

Pour in the cream, stir well, and add the shrimp. Reduce the heat to low and simmer gently, uncovered, until the shrimp turn pink and begin to curl, about 5 minutes. Taste and adjust the seasonings. Serve piping hot.

# Cold White Gazpacho with Grapes
## *Gazpacho Malagueño*

Efrain Martinez, Chef Ef                                                  Serves 4

**Gazpacho is one of the signatures of Spain. On a hot summer day, this fruity Málaga gazpacho will cool you and please you. *¡Viva gazpacho!***

4 cups cold water

4 ounces white bread (or two slices), crusts removed

4 cloves garlic, mashed

2 tablespoons white vinegar

3 tablespoons chopped onion

5 ounces almonds, blanched and chopped, or ¾ cup

¼ teaspoon marjoram leaves

Salt to taste

6 tablespoons virgin olive oil

20 seedless grapes for garnish

3 tablespoons chopped parsley for garnish

In a food processor or blender, place all the ingredients, a little at a time, except the olive oil and the garnish. With the motor running, add the olive oil in a thin stream until smooth. Strain the soup through a wide strainer.

Pour the gazpacho into individual soup bowls and refrigerate. Garnish with the grapes and the chopped parsley and serve chilled.

# Margarita Shrimp Salad

Barbara Pool Fenzl

Serves 4

Every amateur mixologist in the Southwest claims to know the secret to the perfect margarita, the region's popular cocktail made with tequila, Triple Sec, and lime juice. Test their margarita IQ with this spirited shrimp salad to see if they can identify the basics in the dressing. It's a dynamite first course or centerpiece of a summer dinner.

## Shrimp

- 2 tablespoons chopped cilantro
- 2 cloves garlic, minced
- 1 serrano chile, stemmed, seeded, and finely diced
- ⅓ cup tequila
- 2 tablespoons Triple Sec or Grand Marnier
- ¼ cup freshly squeezed lime juice
- 1 teaspoon cumin seed, toasted and ground, or 1 teaspoon ground cumin
- 1 pound shrimp (16 to 20 per pound), peeled, deveined, and slit open along the backs
- ¼ cup olive oil
  Salt and freshly ground black pepper to taste

## Salad

- 4 corn tortillas, 6 inches in diameter, cut into julienne
  Vegetable oil for frying tortillas
- 1 teaspoon chile powder
- 1 tomato, cored, seeded, and diced
- 1 yellow bell pepper, cored, seeded, and diced
- 6 cups torn romaine lettuce leaves, washed and thoroughly dried

## For the shrimp

Combine the cilantro, garlic, chile, tequila, Triple Sec, lime juice, and cumin seed in a nonreactive bowl. Add the shrimp, turn to coat, and refrigerate for at least 1 hour. Drain the shrimp and reserve the marinade.

In a small saucepan over high heat, bring the reserved marinade to a boil. Reduce the heat to medium and simmer until reduced by half. Remove from the heat, transfer to a bowl, and let cool. Whisk in the olive oil and season with salt and pepper to taste. Set aside.

Prepare a barbecue grill or preheat a broiler. Grill or broil the shrimp until just pink, about 1 minute per side. Keep warm.

## For the salad

Fill a small skillet with oil to a depth of about 1 inch and place over medium heat. When the oil is about 375°, fry the tortilla strips in batches until light brown and crisp. Drain on paper towels. Sprinkle with chile powder while still warm.

In a large bowl, mix together the tomato, bell pepper, and lettuce. Toss with the marinade-oil dressing and divide among 4 large plates or shallow bowls. Top the salad with grilled shrimp and fried tortilla strips. Serve immediately.

# Reggae Salad with Pork, Mango, and Orzo

Lynn Fischer — Serves 8 as a side salad or 4 as an entrée

**This salad is a bright and lively island specialty, just like a reggae band. Fresh mango can be found in most supermarkets, but the commercially bottled mango (in the refrigerated section) has lots of taste and is perfectly acceptable. Use it if you want to save the bother of peeling and pitting the fruit.**

**Salad**

Vegetable oil spray

8 ounces pork loin, trimmed of fat

**Dressing**

½ teaspoon chopped pickled jalapeño

2 cups fresh mango diced plus ½ cup diced mango reserved for dressing

2 cloves garlic

3 tablespoons fresh lime juice

⅓ cup fresh orange juice

½ teaspoon cumin

2 tablespoons olive oil

Drop of Tabasco

2 cups cooked orzo or pastita

1 small red bell pepper, minced, plus 2 tablespoons minced red bell pepper, for garnish

½ cup minced red onion plus thinly sliced red onion rings, for garnish

¼ cup chopped cilantro plus 2 tablespoons chopped cilantro, for garnish

Thinly sliced romaine lettuce

Spray a nonstick skillet and heat over medium-high until hot. Sear the pork about 2 minutes per side until quite brown. Reduce the heat and cook until firm to the touch, about 3 minutes per side. Cool and slice into ½-inch by 1-inch strips.

In a food processor or blender, purée the jalapeño, ½ cup mango, garlic, lime juice, orange juice, cumin, olive oil and Tabasco.

In a large bowl, combine the pork, orzo, red pepper, red onion, the remaining mango, and cilantro. Pour the dressing over the pork mixture and toss to mix well. Line a platter or individual plates with romaine. Mound the salad on top and garnish with reserved red pepper, red onion rings, and cilantro. Serve immediately.

# Southwest Salad with Black Beans and Corn

Mollie Katzen · Serves 6 to 8

**Black beans and corn are marinated in olive oil and lots of lime juice and seasoned with garlic, peppers, onion, roasted cumin seeds, and cilantro. Partly chewy, partly crunchy tortilla strips provide textural contrast. This salad keeps extremely well (up to five days or more) if stored in a tightly covered container in the refrigerator. If you are making it a day or two in advance of serving, leave out the fresh cilantro and parsley until a few hours before serving. Also, prepare the tortilla strips as close to serving time as possible. Leftover Southwest Salad makes a wonderful lunch or light supper served cold or at room temperature over hot rice with fresh tortilla chips or quick nachos on the side.**

- 2 cups dried black beans
- 2 cups cooked corn
- 2 to 3 medium-sized cloves garlic, finely minced
- A heaping ½ cup well-minced red onion
- 1 medium-sized red bell pepper, minced
- 1 medium-sized carrot, minced (optional)
- 1 teaspoon salt
- ½ cup extra virgin olive oil (plus an optional 1 to 2 tablespoons for the tortillas)
- ½ cup fresh lime juice (3 to 4 limes)
- 2 to 3 teaspoons whole cumin seeds
- ½ cup minced fresh cilantro
- ½ cup minced fresh parsley
- ½ cup minced fresh basil (if available)
- 1 teaspoon crushed red pepper (adjust this to your taste)
- A moderate amount of freshly ground black pepper
- 3 to 4 corn tortillas (optional)

Soak the beans for at least 4 hours, but preferably overnight. Drain off any excess soaking water, place the soaked beans in a soup pot, and cover with fresh water. Bring *just* to a boil, then cover and turn the heat way down. Cook at a very slow simmer—with no agitation in the water—until the beans are tender. This should take 1¼ to 1½ hours. Check intermittently to be sure there is enough water, and add more if necessary. When the beans are cooked, drain them well. Then rinse them thoroughly in cold water, and drain them well again.

In a large bowl, combine beans, cooked corn, minced garlic, red onion, bell pepper, optional carrot, salt, ½ cup olive oil, and lime juice.

Roast the whole cumin seeds, either in a cast-iron skillet over medium heat, stirring for several minutes,

or very carefully in a toaster oven. Add the toasted seeds to the salad, along with the cilantro, parsley, basil, and red and black pepper, and mix thoroughly but gently.

Lightly brush both sides of each tortilla with olive oil, and cut the tortillas into strips approximately ¼ inch wide and 1½ inches long. Cook the strips slightly by toasting them in an oven (350°) or a toaster oven for only about 2 minutes, or in a heavy skillet over medium heat for 2 to 3 minutes. Ideally, they should be partly crispy and partly chewy. Stir these into the salad shortly before serving, or, if you prefer, scatter them on top as a garnish.

# Tians of Lightly Cured Salmon and Avocado with a Fresh Tomato and Basil Dressing

Rick Stein

Serves 4

**Smoked and raw salmon are shaped into small disks that sandwich slices of avocado. The salmon is flavored with lemon juice, garlic and shallots and accompanied by a sauce of lemon juice, tomato, basil and virgin olive oil. Since the salmon is not cooked, it is essential that it is absolutely fresh. This is not a recipe for making in advance. Everything is just mixed together, molded and then served so that it all tastes of itself. Serve as a first course or maybe as something exceptional to eat outdoors with that special glass of white wine from the Loire.**

4 ounces salmon fillet, skinned

¼ pound smoked salmon

1 large garlic clove, very finely chopped

3 shallots, very finely chopped

1½ tablespoons lemon juice

½ teaspoon salt

12 turns of the black pepper mill

A pinch of cayenne pepper

A few drops of Worcestershire sauce

2 small avocados

Mixed young salad greens, to garnish

**For the Dressing**

4 tablespoons extra-virgin olive oil

1 tablespoon lemon juice

2 tomatoes, peeled, seeded and finely diced

½ teaspoon coarse sea salt

8 fresh basil leaves, very finely shredded

A few turns of the black pepper mill

Thinly slice the salmon fillet and smoked salmon, then cut them into strips about ¼ inch wide. Put them in a bowl with the garlic, shallots, 1 tablespoon of the lemon juice, salt, black pepper, cayenne pepper and Worcestershire sauce and mix together well. Halve the avocados and remove the pit and peel. Cut each half into thin slices, then mix with the remaining lemon juice and a pinch of salt.

Place a 3½-inch poaching ring or plain pastry cutter in the center of each of 4 large plates. Divide half the salmon mixture between the rings and lightly level the top; don't press the mixture down—you want it to be loosely packed. Cover each one with avocado slices and then with the remaining salmon mixture, lightly leveling the top once more. Carefully remove the rings.

Lightly stir the dressing ingredients together in a bowl. Arrange 4 small piles of the salad leaves around each tian. Using a teaspoon, spoon little pools of the dressing in among the leaves and then serve.

# Tomato and Herbed Ricotta Salata Salad

Joanne Weir                                                      Serves 6

**Forty million Americans grow tomatoes, a true testament that picking homegrown tomatoes, warm from the summer sun, is pure joy. Slice and combine them with herbs and ricotta salata, a salted and drained ricotta with a firmer, drier texture than the usual version. More than once, I have been told that this is someone's favorite dish.**

½ pound ricotta salata

2 tablespoons chopped fresh basil

2 tablespoons chopped fresh chives

1 tablespoon chopped fresh mint

1 teaspoon chopped fresh oregano

1 teaspoon chopped fresh thyme

5 large ripe tomatoes, cut into
¼-inch slices

½ pound assorted cherry tomatoes,
red, orange, yellow plum,
green, halved

Salt

¼ cup extra-virgin olive oil

3 tablespoons balsamic vinegar

Freshly ground black pepper

Basil, mint, oregano, and thyme
sprigs as a garnish

Crumble the ricotta salata in a bowl. Add the basil, chives, mint, oregano, and thyme and mix together until all of the herbs stick to the crumbled cheese. Set aside.

Place the sliced tomatoes on a serving platter, overlapping slightly. Scatter the cherry tomatoes on top. Season with salt.

In a small bowl, whisk together the olive oil and vinegar. Season to taste with salt and pepper. Drizzle the vinaigrette onto the tomatoes and let sit for 10 minutes.

To serve, scatter the cheese over the tomatoes and garnish with basil, mint, oregano, and thyme sprigs. Serve immediately.

# Asparagus with Roasted Shallot and Walnut Sauce

Lynn Fischer                                   Serves 4

**Pureed oven-roasted shallots and garlic are the low-fat base to this creamy sauce. I keep a variety of roasted vegetables in the refrigerator to use as quick bases for many different sauces.**

3 to 4 medium shallots, skin on

4 cloves garlic, skin on

Olive oil spray

1 teaspoon fresh lemon juice

4 tablespoons walnuts, toasted and chopped

1 tablespoon canola oil

⅓ cup water or low-sodium vegetable stock

Salt (optional)

Freshly ground black pepper

1 pound fresh asparagus, tough ends discarded

1 teaspoon lemon juice or balsamic vinegar or cider vinegar

Preheat the oven to 350°F.

Line a baking sheet with foil. Place the shallots and garlic on the sheet and lightly spray with oil. Cover with additional foil, crimp the edges, and poke a hole in the top and roast 45 to 50 minutes or until very soft. Set aside until cool enough to handle, then peel. The onions and shallots may be prepared ahead and refrigerated, covered, for up to 4 days.

In a food processor or blender, puree the shallots, garlic, lemon juice, 2 tablespoons of the walnuts, and the oil until smooth. Add the water or stock gradually until it is the desired thickness. Salt, if using, and pepper to taste.

In a small saucepan lightly sprayed with oil, over low heat, cook the shallot mixture, stirring occasionally, until warmed through. Meanwhile, in a large nonstick skillet, heat ½ inch water to boiling. Add the asparagus and reduce heat; cover and simmer for 4 to 6 minutes. Drain and place the asparagus on a serving platter or individual serving plates. Top with the warmed shallot sauce, sprinkle with lemon juice or vinegar, and garnish with the remaining 2 tablespoons of chopped walnuts. Serve immediately.

# Green Tomato Fritters

John Shields

Serves 4

**"Oh my God, what to do with all the tomatoes!"** This was Aunt Catherine's yearly cry each summer when she saw her rows of tomato plants hanging low, weighted down with fruit. One of my all-time favorite ways to use up extra tomatoes is this family recipe: a slightly sweet, spiced batter that makes unbelievably good tomato fritters.

2 large green tomatoes

Milk to cover

1 cup all-purpose flour

2 teaspoons baking powder

½ teaspoon salt

2 eggs, separated

1 teaspoon sugar

⅔ cup milk

Pinch of ground mace

Vegetable oil, for frying

Core the tomatoes and cut into ¼-inch-thick slices. Place in a shallow bowl and add milk to cover. Let stand while making the fritter batter.

Sift together the flour, baking powder, and salt in a bowl. Stir in the egg yolks, sugar, ⅔ cup of milk, and mace. Beat the egg whites until stiff peaks form, then gently fold into the batter.

Pour oil into a skillet to a depth of about 1 inch and heat until very hot, about 375°F. Remove the tomato slices from the milk, dip in batter, and fry, a few at a time, until golden brown on both sides, about 5 minutes. Remove with a slotted utensil to paper towels to drain. Serve hot.

# Dried Cherry Salsa

Barbara Pool Fenzl

Makes about 1½ cups

**The dried cherries are the only "import" in this otherwise all-Southwestern salsa. The other main ingredients are grown in the region. The cherries give the salsa a slightly chewy texture and another layer of fruit. Serve this colorful, toothsome relish with any pork dish for a winning combination.**

¼ cup freshly squeezed orange juice

¼ cup sugar

½ cup coarsely chopped dried cherries

¼ cup coarsely chopped toasted pecans

1 red bell pepper, roasted, peeled, seeded, and diced

1 Anaheim chile, roasted, peeled, seeded, and diced

1 tablespoons grated orange zest

¼ cup chopped cilantro

Salt and freshly ground black pepper to taste

In a small heavy pan over medium heat, bring the orange juice and sugar to a boil, stirring occasionally. Lower the heat and simmer until the sugar is dissolved. Remove from the heat and add the dried cherries. Allow to steep for 1 hour.

In a nonreactive bowl, stir together the remaining ingredients; add the cherry mixture and salt and pepper.

*Do Ahead: The salsa can be made a day ahead of time without the cilantro; add the cilantro just before serving.*

# Oven-Roasted Winter Vegetables

Joanne Weir                                                                      Serves 6

**In the wine country, the soil is so rich and the climate so good that everyone has a garden year round. Winter doesn't necessarily have to mean that fresh vegetables are absent from the table. Instead offer winter root vegetables and tubers—rutabagas, carrots, parsnips—combined with sweet potatoes and Brussels sprouts. Serve with a roasted chicken or as a side dish with your Thanksgiving turkey.**

½ pound rutabagas, peeled and cut into 1-inch pieces

½ pound carrots, peeled and cut into 1-inch pieces

½ pound parsnips, peeled and cut into 1-inch pieces

½ pound Brussels sprouts, trimmed

½ pound sweet potatoes, peeled and cut into 1-inch pieces

1 tablespoon unsalted butter

1 tablespoon extra-virgin olive oil

2 teaspoons chopped fresh thyme

2 teaspoons chopped fresh sage

⅛ teaspoon freshly grated nutmeg

Salt and freshly ground black pepper

½ cup Marsala

Preheat the oven to 450°F.

Bring a pot of salted water to a boil. Add the rutabagas, carrots, and parsnips and simmer until they give slightly when pierced with a fork, about 5 minutes.

Place the rutabagas, carrots, parsnips, Brussels sprouts, and sweet potatoes in a large roasting pan. Melt the butter in a small saucepan and stir in the oil, thyme, sage, and nutmeg. Drizzle the butter mixture over the vegetables and toss to coat them completely. Season to taste with salt and pepper. Pour the Marsala into the bottom of the roasting pan. Cover tightly with foil and bake in the oven for 40 minutes. Remove the foil, toss the vegetables, and continue to cook until the Marsala is evaporated and the vegetables can be easily pierced with a knife, 20 to 30 minutes.

Place the roasted vegetables on a platter and serve immediately.

# Celery Root and Pear Puree

Todd English                                                                    Serves 4

1 large celery root (celeriac), peeled and cut into 1 inch cubes

½ large white onion, diced

2 ripe pears (Bosc, Anjou or Bartlett are good), peeled, cored and diced

¾ cup heavy cream

3 tablespoons unsalted butter

1–2 teaspoons kosher salt

½ teaspoon black pepper

Place the celery root, onion and pears in a small saucepan and bring to boil over high heat. Lower the heat to medium low and cook until the celery root is very soft, about 50 minutes. Drain, reserving 1/2 cup of the cooking liquid.

Place the celery root mixture in a blender or food processor fitted with a steel blade and process until smooth. Add the cream, butter, salt and pepper and pulse to combine. If necessary, reheat over low heat. The mixture should be almost souplike. If necessary, add the reserved cooking liquid. Add the salt and pepper.

# Penne au Gratin

Jacques Pépin

Serves 4

**This satisfying dish is a variation of the old favorite, macaroni and cheese. Although the cream sauce is traditionally made with milk and cream, I use only whole milk in this recipe, and the result is quite velvety and rich. To reduce the calorie count even further, use skim milk instead of whole milk.**

6 ounces penne pasta (2¼ cups)

1½ teaspoons unsalted butter

1 tablespoon virgin olive oil

2 tablespoons all-purpose flour

2½ cups milk

4½ ounces cheddar cheese, cut into ½-inch dice (1 cup)

¾ teaspoon salt

¾ teaspoon freshly ground black pepper

1 large tomato (8 ounces), halved, seeded, and the flesh cut into ½-inch dice (1¼ cups)

1½ tablespoons grated Parmesan cheese

½ teaspoon paprika

Bring 2½ quarts of water to a boil in a pot. Add the penne, bring the water back to a boil, and boil the pasta over medium heat, uncovered, for about 8 minutes. (The pasta should be *al dente*, firm to the bite.) Drain the penne in a colander, rinse it under cold tap water until cool, and set it aside.

Heat the butter and oil in a saucepan, and add the flour. Cook the mixture over medium heat for about 10 seconds, then add the milk, and stir it in quickly with a whisk so the mixture doesn't scorch. Bring the mixture to a boil, and boil it for 10 seconds. Add the cheddar cheese, salt, and pepper, mix well, then cook over low heat for 3 to 4 minutes. Set aside.

When ready to finish the gratin, preheat the oven to 400 degrees.

Mix the pasta with the cheddar sauce, and transfer the mixture to a 6-cup gratin dish. Sprinkle the tomato on top of the pasta and sauce. Combine the Parmesan and paprika in a small bowl, and sprinkle the mixture on the pasta. Bake in the 400-degree oven for 30 minutes, until the gratin is bubbly and nicely browned on top. Serve immediately.

*Note: If making the gratin at the last moment, and assembling it while the sauce and pasta are both hot, do not bake the gratin. Instead, place it under a hot broiler until golden brown on top.*

# Vegetarian Fried Rice

Tommy Tang

**You mix the vegetables and throw in the rice. What could be easier?**

3 tablespoons olive oil

1½ teaspoons finely chopped garlic

3 ounces small broccoli florets (about 1 cup)

¾ cup sliced onions

⅔ cup sliced snow peas

⅔ cup diced tomatoes

¼ cup diced mushrooms

¼ cup julienned carrots

¼ cup diced celery

¼ cup diced red bell pepper

4 cups cooked white or brown rice

2 tablespoons oyster sauce

1½ tablespoons Thai fish sauce

1 teaspoon black pepper

2 tablespoons diced scallions

¼ cup thinly sliced leeks

Heat olive oil in a large skillet over high heat. Add garlic and sauté until lightly browned, about 1 minute. Add broccoli, onions, snow peas, tomatoes, mushrooms, carrots, celery, and bell pepper and stir-fry 1 minute. Add rice, oyster sauce, fish sauce, and black pepper and cook, stirring constantly, 3 minutes. Transfer to a platter, sprinkle with scallions and leeks, and serve.

# The Stove-Top Anna

Julia Child                                      Makes 6 servings

**This is a frying-pan take-off on the famous Potatoes Anna, in which a mold of sliced potatoes is baked in a hot oven and then unmolded like a cake. The classic Anna is a spectacular dish, a *tour de force*. The Stove-Top Anna, on the other hand, is not much of a trick provided you have the right frying pan. You will note here that you may include slices of Swiss cheese if you wish, and it could then be a luncheon or supper main course to serve with fried or poached eggs and/or a green salad.**

2½ pounds "boiling" potatoes (about 10 cups, sliced)

⅓ to ½ cup clarified butter or olive oil

4 ounces Swiss cheese, cut into slices ⅛ inch thick and about 1 by 1½ inches across (to make 1 cup), optional

Salt and freshly ground pepper

Freshly grated nutmeg

### Preparing the potatoes

One at a time, peel the potatoes and cut into fairly neat round slices 1¼ inches in diameter and ¼ inch thick. Drop them, as you do so, into a bowl of cold water. When all are done, drain the slices, and dry in a towel.

### Preliminary cooking

Pour ¼ inch of clarified butter or olive oil into the frying pan, set over moderate heat, and rapidly arrange an overlapping layer of potato slices in the pan, shaking it gently from time to time to prevent sticking. Baste with a sprinkling of butter or oil, arrange a second layer over the first, and over this arrange a layer of the optional cheese slices. Season a third layer of potatoes with salt, pepper, and a speck of nutmeg. Continue filling the pan with potatoes, optional cheese, seasonings, and end with a layer of potatoes. When filled, shake the pan gently

again, and let cook 3 to 5 minutes over moderately high heat to be sure the bottom is crusting.

### Finishing the cooking

Then cover the pan and set over low heat for 45 minutes, or until the potatoes are tender when pierced with a small knife. (Be sure the heat is regulated so that the potatoes do not burn on the bottom.) Run a spatula all around the edge of the pan and underneath the potatoes to loosen them; unmold onto a hot serving dish.

*Ahead-of-time Note: If done somewhat in advance, cover the potatoes loosely and keep in a warming oven or over almost-simmering water —they must have air circulation, and they must stay warm to retain their freshly cooked taste.*

*Special Equipment Suggested: A heavy 10-inch no-stick frying pan, or a very well seasoned cast-iron pan; a cover for the pan.*

# Main Courses— Fish and Seafood

## WITH PAUL PRUDHOMME

Paul Prudhomme's name is synonymous with Louisiana cuisine. Born in Acadiana country, the youngest of thirteen children, Paul grew up in a house without electricity. Lacking refrigeration, the family prepared only enough for each day's meals, depending on the bounty of the bayous and the year-round vegetable plot for sustenance and inspiration. Paul knew from an early age that he wanted to go into the restaurant business, so he traveled and apprenticed at kitchens all over the country. He eventually made his way back to New Orleans, where in 1979 he opened K-Paul's Louisiana Kitchen with his wife, Kay. Two decades later, visitors from all over the world come to sample his blackened fish and other signature fare.

Paul's flavor-blasted food, with its complex combinations of (not always incendiary) spices, woke up America's taste buds. Cajun cooking became a national rage almost overnight, and our love affair with spicy foods continues today. Paul's *Fork in the Road* public television series showed viewers how zesty seasoning gives reduced-fat foods so much oomph you'll never miss the calories. His latest, *Kitchen Expedition,* is a collection of recipes culled from his gastronomic adventures from around the world. You can be sure that his seafood dishes here will not be timidly spiced.

# Sesame Crusted Fish

Paul Prudhomme                                                           Serves 4

### Seasoning Mix

- 2 tablespoons plus 1 teaspoon Chef Paul Prudhomme's Seafood Magic
- ¼ teaspoon ground anise
- ¼ teaspoon ground cinnamon
- 4 fillets of fresh drum (or other firm fleshed fish), about 3 to 4 ounces each
- Peanut oil (preferred) or vegetable oil, for frying

### Battering

- 1 large egg
- 1 tablespoon heavy cream
- ¼ cup sesame seeds
- ½ cup yellow cornmeal

### Sauce

- 2 tablespoons all-purpose flour
- 1 cup white grape juice
- 2 teaspoons fresh lemon juice
- 2 teaspoons fresh lime juice
- 1 tablespoon soy sauce
- 2 teaspoons Magic Pepper Sauce (optional)
- 1 tablespoon light brown sugar

**For the seasoning mix**

Blend together the seasoning mix. Season the drum fillets evenly with 2 teaspoons per side of the mix.

Fill a 12-inch skillet with the oil to a depth of ½ inch. Place over high heat and bring the temperature of the oil to 350°. While the oil is heating, prepare the wet and dry batters.

**For the battering**

Place the egg and cream in a 4x4-inch casserole dish (or any similar dish with sides.) Whisk until well combined. In a similar dish, combine the sesame seeds, cornmeal, and 1¾ teaspoons of the seasoning mix.

When the oil is ready, place the drum pieces in the wet batter and turn until coated on all sides. (Do not discard the wet batter—you will use it later in the recipe.) Transfer the pieces, a few at a time, to the dry batter. Mound the dry batter over the fish pieces and press in with your hands until the pieces are evenly coated. Gently shake off the excess and transfer immediately to the hot oil.

Fry the pieces, turning them several times, until they are light golden brown on both sides, about 6 to 7 minutes. Drain on paper towels and keep warm while you make the sauce.

**For the sauce**

Pour out all but 1 tablespoon of the oil from the skillet. Return the skillet to high heat and add the flour. Whisk constantly until flour is mocha colored, about 2 minutes. Add the grape juice, lemon juice, lime juice, soy sauce, Magic Pepper Sauce, brown sugar, and the remaining seasoning mix. Bring to a boil, whisking constantly, then add the reserved egg/cream mixture. Whisk in well, remove the skillet from the heat and continue to whisk constantly until the mixture has cooled down slightly, about 30 seconds. You should have about 1¼ cups of sauce.

Serve 1 fish fillet per person, accompanied by ¼ cup of the sauce.

# Roasted Spice Rubbed Striped Bass on a Bed of Chickpeas with a Fresh Tomato Salad

Todd English                                                                Serves 4

## For the Bass

- 3 garlic cloves, sliced or roughly chopped
- 1 tablespoon fresh rosemary leaves
- 1 tablespoon Hungarian paprika
- 2 tablespoons turmeric
- 1 tablespoon curry powder
- 2 teaspoons ground cumin
- 1 teaspoon ground ginger
- 1 teaspoon kosher salt
- ½ teaspoon black pepper
- ¼ cup olive oil
- 2 to 2½ pounds striped bass

## For the Chickpeas

- 1 tablespoon olive oil
- ½ Spanish onion, chopped
- 2 garlic cloves, chopped
- ½ fennel bulb, cut in small dice
- 1 large carrot, cut in small dice
- 1 teaspoon fresh rosemary leaves
- ¼ to ½ teaspoon red pepper flakes
- 2 cups cooked chickpeas, rinsed
- 1 to 1½ cups chicken broth
- ½ cup white wine

## For the Tomato Salad

- 2 beefsteak tomatoes, cut in medium dice
- 1 tablespoon extra virgin olive oil
- 1 to 2 teaspoons fresh lemon juice
- 1 tablespoon chopped fresh basil leaves
- 1 tablespoon chopped fresh cilantro leaves
- ½ teaspoon kosher salt
- ¼ teaspoon black pepper
- 2 sprigs fresh basil, for garnish
- 2 sprigs fresh parsley, for garnish

## To prepare the fish

Place the garlic and rosemary in a food processor fitted with a steel blade and pulse. Add the spices, salt and pepper and pulse until well chopped. Gradually, while the machine is running, add the olive oil and blend until it forms a paste. Coat the fish with the paste, cover and refrigerate at least 20 minutes and no longer than 4 hours.

## To prepare the chickpeas

Place a large cast iron or oven-proof skillet over a medium heat and when it is hot, add the oil. Add the onion, garlic, fennel, carrot, rosemary and red pepper flakes, stirring well after each addition, and cook until the onion is soft and lightly golden, about 7–10 minutes. Add the chickpeas and chicken broth and cook until heated through, about 3–5 minutes. Leave the mixture in the skillet.

## To make the tomato salad

Place the tomatoes, basil, cilantro, salt and pepper in a bowl and mix to combine. Set aside.

Preheat the oven to 425 degrees.

## To roast the fish

Remove excess paste from the fish, place the fish on top of the chickpeas and drizzle the wine around the sides. Transfer the fish to the oven and roast until the inside is white and tender, about 15–20 minutes, depending on the thickness. Divide the chickpeas between four shallow bowls, top with equal amounts of fish and equal amounts of tomato salad and serve immediately.

# Pepper-Encrusted Salmon with Green Sauce

Caprial Pence                                    Serves 6

**After growing up eating wild salmon, I can't get terribly excited about the farmed variety. My favorite is still wild Copper River salmon, which has such a good flavor that it can stand up to all the pepper and the sauce in this recipe. The sauce can be kept in the refrigerator for up to a week. If you prefer, you can grill the salmon after dredging it in the pepper.**

**Green Sauce**

1 bunch fresh parsley, coarsely chopped

1 bunch fresh basil, coarsely chopped

1 tablespoon coarsely chopped fresh mint

4 cloves garlic, chopped

2 heaping tablespoons chopped capers

4 oil- or salt-packed anchovies, chopped

Zest of 1 lemon

2 tablespoons freshly squeezed lemon juice

⅔ cup extra virgin olive oil

Salt

Freshly ground black pepper

6 (6-ounce) salmon fillets

1 tablespoon cracked black peppercorns

1 tablespoon cracked green peppercorns

1 tablespoon cracked pink peppercorns

Kosher salt

1 tablespoon extra virgin olive oil or vegetable oil

To prepare the sauce, combine the parsley, basil, and mint in a large bowl. Add the garlic, capers, anchovies, lemon zest, and lemon juice and whisk to combine. Slowly whisk in the olive oil and season to taste with salt and pepper. Set aside. (If not using right away, cover and refrigerate. Bring the sauce to room temperature at least 20 to 30 minutes before using.)

To prepare the salmon, preheat the oven to 350°. Combine the black, green, and pink peppercorns in a small bowl. Season the salmon with the kosher salt and coat with the peppercorn mixture. Heat the olive oil in a very large ovenproof sauté pan over high heat until smoking hot. Add the salmon fillets and sear both sides well, about 2 minutes. Put the pan in the oven and bake for 5 to 7 minutes, depending on the thickness of the fillets. To test for doneness, insert a skewer in the fish, then remove it and touch the tip to your lip; if it is warm, the fish is done. Alternatively, grill fillets on a hot grill for about 4 minutes on each side. Remove the pan from the oven and place the fish on a serving platter. Spoon the sauce over the top of each piece of salmon and serve hot.

# Trout Praline

John D. Folse

Serves 6

6 (5- to 8-ounce) trout fillets

¾ cup vegetable oil

Egg wash (1 egg, ½ cup water,
½ cup milk, blended)

1 cup pecan flour

½ cup flour

1 tablespoon diced garlic

½ cup sliced green onions

¾ cup chopped pecans

1½ ounces Frangelico liqueur

2 cups heavy whipping cream

4 pats cold butter

¼ cup chopped parsley

Salt and black pepper

Louisiana Gold Pepper Sauce or
other Louisiana hot sauce

You may purchase pecan flour from any specialty bake shop. Combine pecan flour and flour in a small mixing bowl. Season to taste using salt and pepper. In a 10-inch cast iron skillet, heat oil over medium-high heat. Dip fillets in egg wash and coat generously with flour. Sauté fillets in hot oil until golden brown, 3–5 minutes on each side. Once done, remove from skillet and keep warm. In the same skillet, place garlic, green onions and pecans. Sauté 3–5 minutes or until vegetables are wilted. Deglaze with Frangelico and add heavy whipping cream. Bring to a low boil and simmer until cream is reduced by ½ volume. Add cold butter, two pats at a time, swirling pan constantly until all is incorporated. Butter will finish sauce to a nice sheen. Add parsley and season to taste using salt, pepper and Louisiana Gold. Place sauce in the center of a serving plate and top with trout fillet.

# Tuna Steaks with Tapenade Coating

Jacques Pépin                                                    Serves 4

**This recipe is excellent when prepared with tuna, but it's good, too, made with other fish that will hold their shape when sautéed in a skillet. I use small but fairly thick steaks, covering each with *tapenade*, a mixture of different types of olives, capers, anchovy fillets, and garlic. For maximum flavor transfer, I cook the steaks *tapenade* side down over high heat to start.**

**Tapenade**

¼ cup pitted Kalamata olives

¼ cup oil-cured olives

2 tablespoons drained capers

3 anchovy fillets (packed in oil)

1 large clove garlic, peeled

1 pound yellowfin tuna (center cut), completely cleaned of all sinew (about 5 inches long and 2½ to 3 inches in diameter)

1 tablespoon canola oil

½ teaspoon salt

1 cup arugula leaves, cleaned

**For the tapenade**
Place all the *tapenade* ingredients in the bowl of a small food processor, and process until finely chopped but not pureed. Makes about ½ cup.

Cut the tuna into 4 equal-size pieces, each about 1 inch thick and 2½ to 3 inches in diameter. Cover the top of each steak with 2 tablespoons of the *tapenade* mixture, patting it firmly over the surface of the steak.

At serving time, preheat the oven to 180 degrees.

Heat the tablespoon of oil until hot in a large skillet. Place the steaks *tapenade* side down in the hot skillet, and sprinkle them with the salt. Cover, and cook the steaks over high heat for about 1½ minutes. Turn them over, *tapenade* side up, cover, and cook for another 1½ minutes over medium to high heat.

Transfer the steaks to an ovenproof platter, and warm them in the 180-degree oven for at least 5 to 10 minutes but up to 30 minutes. Serve the steaks whole or sliced, surrounded by the arugula leaves.

# Red Snapper Fillets with Shrimp, Tomatoes, and Zucchini
## Filets de Rouget aux Crevettes, Tomates, et Courgettes

Pierre Franey                                                    Serves 4

**In honor of the Côte d'Azur, I put together my own seafood and vegetable recipe.**

4 small red snapper fillets, about ¼ pound each, skin on

8 jumbo shrimp (6 to the pound), peeled and deveined

Salt and freshly ground pepper to taste

½ cup flour

4 tablespoons olive oil

1 tablespoon finely chopped shallots

1 cup ripe tomato, peeled, seeded, and cut into 1-inch cubes

1 cup zucchini, cut into fine strips about 1½ inches long

1 tablespoon red wine vinegar

1 tablespoon black or green olives, pitted and chopped

3 tablespoons flat green parsley, finely chopped

Sprinkle the fish and shrimp with salt and pepper to taste and then dip them in flour, shaking off the excess.

Heat 2 tablespoons of the oil over high heat in a nonstick skillet large enough to hold the fish in one layer. Add the fish skin side down and cook for 3 minutes or until lightly brown. Turn and cook for about 3 minutes more, or until done. Remove and keep warm.

In the same skillet, add the shrimp and cook briefly on both sides until done. Remove and keep warm.

In the same skillet, heat the remaining olive oil. Add the shallots and cook briefly until wilted. Add the tomato, zucchini, and salt and pepper to taste, and cook over high heat, stirring and tossing, for about 3 minutes. Add the vinegar and the olives and cook, stirring, for another minute. Blend in the 3 tablespoons of parsley.

To serve, divide this mixture onto 4 plates and place the fish fillets and shrimp on top. Sprinkle with remaining parsley.

# Mahimahi with Orange and Cilantro

George Hirsch                                                   Serves 4

**Mahimahi is very popular in Hawaii and the Pacific Northwest, and its reputation for being a tasty fish is slowly making its way toward the East Coast. This simple dish gets its sweetness from the orange and its pungency from the cilantro.**

½ cup fresh orange juice

½ cup olive oil

½ cup orange segments

2 tablespoons chopped cilantro

3 scallions, chopped fine

¼ cup white wine

¼ teaspoon Tabasco sauce

¼ teaspoon Worcestershire sauce

Four 8-ounce mahimahi fillets

Combine the orange juice, olive oil, orange segments, cilantro, scallion, white wine, Tabasco, and Worcestershire sauce in a shallow bowl and mix well. Marinate the fish in this mixture for at least 1 hour in the refrigerator. Place the fish and

the marinade in a nonstick skillet and grill for 4 to 5 minutes. Remove the fish and set it aside. Reduce the marinade and pour it over the fish.

*Grill Temperature: Medium*

# Poached Salmon with Noodles, Fennel, and Apple

Charlie Trotter

Serves 4

**Of all the fish and shellfish that can be poached, salmon probably enjoys the easiest, most splendid results. In this dish, the poaching liquid is used as the broth, which not only provides great flavor but it is also quite healthy. The apple and fennel add pleasurable notes of sweetness and texture helping to make the final combination of flavors, aromas, and textures both earthy and elegant. Any type or quantity of noodles can be used, or perhaps even rice, making this dish easy to serve as an appetizer or an entrée.**

½ cup chopped carrots

½ cup chopped celery

½ cup chopped Spanish onion

½ cup chopped Granny Smith apple

½ cup chopped leeks

1 tablespoon black peppercorns

2 bay leaves

2 quarts water

½ cup fresh tarragon leaves

8 ounces dried fettuccini noodles, cooked and tossed with 2 tablespoons olive oil

1½ cups cremini mushrooms, cleaned and sliced

1 bulb fennel, julienned

4 4-ounce pieces salmon

Salt and pepper

1 Granny Smith apple, julienned

¼ cup coarsely chopped fennel tops

8 teaspoons olive oil

## Method

To make the broth: Place the carrots, celery, onion, the chopped apple, leeks, black peppercorns, and bay leaves in a medium saucepan, cover with water, and simmer over medium heat for 30 minutes. Add the tarragon and continue to cook for 2 minutes. Strain the mixture through a fine-mesh sieve, return the broth to the saucepan, and bring to a simmer.

To reheat the noodles: Use a wide, shallow sieve to warm the noodles in the broth and then place them in a bowl.

To prepare the vegetables: Place the sliced mushrooms and julienned fennel in the broth, heat for 2 minutes, and remove from the broth.

To poach the salmon: Place the salmon in the broth and cook for 2 to 4 minutes, or until cooked medium. Remove the salmon and season with salt and pepper. Season the broth to taste with salt and pepper.

## Assembly

Place some of the noodles, mushrooms, fennel, and julienned apple in the center of each bowl. Top with the salmon and ladle in some of the broth. Sprinkle some of the fennel tops around the bowl and drizzle some of the olive oil around the broth. Top with freshly ground black pepper.

*Wine Notes: A lean, crisp-style Sauvignon Blanc like Babcock "Eleven Oaks" from Santa Barbara will be perfect for this dish. The delicate citrus flavors play well with the salmon and apple, and the light fennel flavors of the Sauvignon Blanc really enhance those from the dish.*

# Fillets of Flounder with Pancetta and Beurre Noisette

Rick Stein                                                     Serves 4

**This incredibly simple dish relies on presentation for its effect. The fillets of fish are arranged down the center of a nice oval serving dish, interleaved with thin slices of fried pancetta or, if you can't get it, extremely thinly sliced bacon. It looks wonderful when surrounded with *beurre noisette*, which is simply butter heated until brown and nutty smelling, then sharpened with lemon juice. Next time you're in France and wandering through a market, do make sure you buy one of those long, narrow, elegant, white oval fish dishes for presenting food like this. Owing to the demise of silver service in restaurants, it is all too rare to see dishes served up in a formal manner from the kitchen, but if it's done well it is extremely effective. I suspect that, as everything in restaurant cooking appears to be of a cyclical nature, the era of presenting beautiful large platters of food at the table will return.**

16 small, very thin slices pancetta or 8 thin slices bacon, halved

2 tablespoons sunflower oil

3 tablespoons unsalted butter

3 tablespoons all-purpose flour

½ teaspoon salt

10 turns of the white pepper mill

8 flounder fillets, weighing about 3 to 4 ounces each, skinned

Juice of ¼ lemon

2 teaspoons chopped fresh *fines herbes* (parsley, chervil, chives and tarragon)

Preheat the broiler. Broil the slices of pancetta or bacon for 1 to 1½ minutes on each side, or until crisp. Set aside and keep warm.

Heat the oil and 1 tablespoon of the butter in a large frying pan. Season the flour with the salt and white pepper and spread it over a large plate. Cut each fish fillet across in half and then dip the pieces in the seasoned flour. Fry for 2 minutes on each side, or until lightly golden, then arrange them down the center of a warmed oval serving platter, interleaving them with the slices of grilled pancetta or bacon.

Discard the frying oil, add the remaining butter and allow it to melt over medium heat. When the butter starts to smell nutty and turn light brown, quickly add the lemon juice and herbs and then pour it right over the fish and bacon. Serve straight away.

# Fillet of Sole with Provençal Flavors

Madeleine Kamman                                    Serves 6

**This is an old-fashioned method of cooking fish. It's quite nice for a small dinner party.**

3  tablespoons and ½ cup butter

½  pound sliced mushrooms

   Salt

   Freshly ground pepper

1  teaspoon orange rind, finely grated

¼  teaspoon lemon rind, finely grated

1  teaspoon powdered dry basil

6  large sole fillets

½  cup fish fumet or bottled clam juice

¼  cup dry white wine

¼  cup heavy cream

⅛  teaspoon powdered saffron

1½  tablespoons slivered orange and lime rind, blanched

Heat 1 tablespoon of the butter in a skillet. Add the mushrooms and sauté them. Salt and pepper them, cover the pan and let the juices escape. Cool completely.

Butter a baking dish with 2 tablespoons of butter. Add the mushrooms, the grated orange and lemon rind and the basil and arrange the sole fillets on top. Mix the fish fumet or clam juice with the white wine and pour over the fillets. Cover the fillets with a sheet of parchment paper. Bake in a preheated 375° oven for 8 minutes. Remove the fish from the oven. Keep the fillets warm between two plates so they finish cooking while you make your sauce.

Drain the cooking juices and mushrooms from the baking pan into a skillet. Bring the sauce to a boil. Add the cream, then the ½ cup of butter. Correct the seasoning. Add the saffron.

Serve the fillets on a bed of the mushroom sauce and top with a mixture of the blanched slivers of orange and lime rinds.

# Fish Tacos from Baja California

Rick Stein

Serves 4

I've never been to Baja California in Mexico, but I got the idea for this recipe from the television presenter and food journalist, Hugh Fearnley-Whittingstall, who lent me a book on Baja because I'm very keen on surfing and the waves there are fantastic. He told me about this great dish consisting of a tortilla filled with deep-fried fish, cilantro, chili, tomato, a little sour cream and some salad. I knocked it all up according to how it sounded to me and it's brilliant. One day I'll make the trip to Ensenada with my big old Malibu and ride the odd small wave that may just happen down there.

- 2 sea bream or sea bass, weighing about 2¾ pounds each, filleted
- Salt and freshly ground black pepper
- 8 flour tortillas
- ½ pound iceberg lettuce, finely shredded
- 1¼ cups sour cream
- Sunflower oil for deep-frying

**For the Batter**

- 1⅔ cups all-purpose flour
- 2 eggs
- ⅞ cup water

**For the Salsa**

- 1 medium red onion, finely chopped
- 5 tomatoes, peeled, seeded and finely chopped
- 3 or 4 red chilies, seeded and finely chopped
- 1 teaspoon sugar
- Juice of 1 lime
- 4 tablespoons chopped fresh cilantro
- Salt

First make the salsa by mixing together all the ingredients with a pinch of salt. Set aside.

Cut the fish fillets across into strips ½ inch wide and season with plenty of salt and pepper. For the batter, put the flour, eggs, water and a pinch of salt into a blender and blend until smooth.

Pour the sunflower oil into a pan until it is about one-third full and heat to 375°F, or until a small piece of white bread dropped into the oil browns and rises to the surface in 1 minute. Warm the tortillas in a low oven or a microwave.

Dip the strips of fish into the batter and then drop them into the hot oil and fry for 4 minutes, or until crisp and golden. Lift out with a slotted spoon and drain briefly on paper towels.

To serve, put some lettuce down the center of each tortilla, top with the fried fish, then spoon over some salsa and sour cream. Fold in the sides, roll up as tightly as you can and serve straight away, with some cold Mexican beer.

# Seafood-Smothered Potatoes

### Paul Prudhomme

**If you prefer, you can use all chicken stock or all fish stock instead of the two different stocks. And you certainly can use all one color of bell peppers, instead of the three colors, but I like the way the three colors look. I really like this dish too—it goes great with just about any kind of seafood, and is wonderful all by itself! This recipe is completely traditional, with nothing new to it—just typical south Louisiana fare. It's a perfect example of not fixing something that's not broken.**

1 tablespoon plus 1 teaspoon olive oil

1½ cups chopped onions, in all

¾ cup chopped green bell peppers, in all

¾ cup chopped red bell peppers, in all

¾ cup chopped yellow bell peppers, in all

1 tablespoon plus 1½ teaspoons Chef Paul Prudhomme's Seafood Magic

1½ cups fish stock, in all

1½ cups chicken stock, in all

1½ teaspoons minced fresh garlic

1½ pounds white potatoes, peeled and cut into ½-inch pieces

1½ pounds white potatoes, peeled and cut into 1-inch pieces

½ pound peeled raw shrimp, (21–25 shrimp per pound), about 1 pound unpeeled

1 pint raw oysters in their liquid

½ pound crabmeat, picked over to remove pieces of shell and cartilage

Heat the oil in a heavy 4-quart pot, preferably nonstick, over high heat just until it begins to smoke, about 3 to 4 minutes. Add 1 cup of the onions, ½ cup of each color bell pepper, and 1 teaspoon of Seafood Magic. Cover and cook, uncovering every 2 minutes to stir and scrape the bottom of the pot, until the color of the vegetables has faded and they are just beginning to brown, about 6 to 8 minutes.

Add ½ cup of the fish stock and the remaining Seafood Magic. Stir, re-cover, and cook, uncovering every 2 minutes to stir, until the mixture begins to stick to the bottom of the pot, about 4 to 6 minutes. Uncover and add ½ cup chicken stock, then scrape the bottom of the pot well to loosen any of the brown bits and dissolve them into the liquid. Re-cover and cook until the mixture begins to stick again, about 3 to 4 minutes. Uncover and stir in the remaining onions, the remaining bell peppers, and the garlic. Re-cover and cook until the liquid has almost evaporated and what remains has tiny steam vent holes all over the surface, about 4 minutes. Scrape the bottom well, loosening any brown bits that stick to the bottom. Re-cover and cook for 2 more minutes, then uncover and add ½ cup fish stock. Cook uncovered, stirring every 2 minutes and scraping the bottom of the pot, until the vegetables are soft and have absorbed color from the seasoning mix and the liquid has almost evaporated, about 8 to 10 minutes. Add the remaining ½ cup fish stock and the remaining 1 cup chicken stock. The liquid is a beautiful deep brown and the vegetables are brightly colored, but the taste is very bitter at this point, with a very high level of seasonings, overpowering the milder vegetable taste.

Scrape the bottom well, then add the potatoes. Stir well and cover, then reduce the heat to medium. Cook, uncovering every 5 minutes to stir and scrap the bottom of the pot, until the potatoes are fully cooked and soft, and the sauce is very thick, about 35 to 40 minutes. During this time there will be a lot of bubbling going on! And the potatoes will be so soft that they will begin to disintegrate and thicken the liquid—but that's great because they add wonderful flavor and texture.

At the end of the 35 to 40 minutes the sauce has a faint seafood taste, and a light brown gravy flavor is softened by the starchy potato taste, which spreads across the tongue. The seasonings are still pronounced.

Now add the shrimp, oysters, crabmeat, and oyster liquid. Cover and cook just until the seafood is cooked through but still tender, about 3 to 4 minutes. Watch the shrimp as a guide—they will become plump and opaque when they're done—and don't overcook, or they'll be tough. The final appearance is very much like a stew, and the final taste is of fully balanced potato and seafood gravy flavors. Serve piping hot.

# Hot and Spicy Calamari
## *Calamari all'Arrabbiata*

Giuliano Bugialli                                     Serves 4 to 6

---

Fried calamari in tomato sauce with hot red pepper is one of the most classic ways of preparing it. The dish is most characteristic of the Naples area, though it shares the combination of ingredients with Calabria as well. Italians coat calamari very lightly, often just throwing a little flour over it and shaking the colander to remove any excess, as is common in Tuscany. The next lightest coating, as in this recipe, is to dip it in egg after being lightly floured. If the oil is hot enough, the coating should seal instantly and not allow oil to enter, resulting in fried calamari that is crisp, very light, and not greasy. When frying is heavy and unhealthy, it is usually because the cook doesn't know how to fry properly. In the mid-twentieth century, it became accepted wisdom that it was better to fry with seed vegetable oils than with olive oil, the latter being too heavy. A little olive oil was sometimes included just for flavor. But opinion seems to be changing now, and olive oil is coming back for frying, its supposed heaviness having been revealed as a bit of a myth.

---

1½ pounds small calamari, cleaned

1 lemon, cut in half

Coarse-grained salt

**For the Tomato Sauce**

2 pounds ripe tomatoes or canned tomatoes, preferably imported Italian

¼ cup extra virgin olive oil

4 large cloves garlic, peeled

1 large yellow onion, cleaned and thinly sliced

Salt and freshly ground black pepper

Hot red pepper flakes

**To Cook the Calamari**

2 cups vegetable oil (½ sunflower oil and ½ corn oil)

1 cup extra virgin olive oil

3 extra-large eggs

Pinch of salt

About 1½ cups unbleached all-purpose flour

**To Serve**

20 sprigs fresh Italian parsley, leaves only

3 large cloves garlic, peeled and chopped

Cut the stomach of the calamari into about 1-inch-thick rings. Squeeze the lemon halves into a bowl of cold water, add the salt and the calamari, and soak for half an hour.

Meanwhile, prepare the sauce. If fresh tomatoes are used, cut them into large pieces. Place the fresh or canned tomatoes, olive oil, and garlic in a medium-size nonreactive skillet set over medium heat. Cook, stirring with a wooden spoon every so often. Soak the onion slices in a bowl of cold water for 15 minutes, drain, and add to the tomato sauce. Season with salt and black and red pepper. Cook until onions are translucent and almost fully cooked, but not overcooked, adding a little lukewarm water if the sauce becomes too dry. The tomatoes should not be allowed to fall completely apart. Finely chop the parsley and garlic together on a cutting board.

When ready, drain the calamari rings, rinse them under cold running water, and pat them dry with paper towels. Heat the vegetable oil and olive oil together in a deep-fryer or large skillet over medium heat. Use a fork to very lightly beat the eggs together with the salt in a small bowl. When the oil is hot, about 400 degrees, put the calamari in a large colander, pour the flour over the calamari, and vigorously shake the colander to remove the excess flour. Dip each piece of fish in the beaten eggs, then add to the hot oil. Add enough calamari to have only one layer in the skillet. Cook until the rings are golden all over, 3 to 4 minutes for small calamari. Use a slotted spoon to transfer them to a platter lined with paper towels in order to remove excess oil. Repeat with the remainder.

Arrange the tomato sauce on a large platter, transfer the calamari onto it, then sprinkle with the parsley leaves and garlic and serve hot.

# Lobster with Latkas

Jennifer Paterson and Clarissa Dickson Wright, Two Fat Ladies

I have an unlimited passion for lobsters, which I do very well with, thanks to my dear Mr. Clarke of Fisher Row, Musselburgh, the best fishmonger in Britain. I also love latkas, those crispy mouth-watering Jewish potato pancakes. So it seemed to me an excellent idea to combine the two. CDW

4 boiled lobsters

6 tablespoons (¾ stick) butter

Scant 1 cup sliced shallots

2 cups sliced mushrooms

⅔ cup whiskey

Freshly ground black pepper

Pinch of ground cloves

1¼ cups heavy cream

**For the Latkas**

2 pounds potatoes, peeled and finely grated

1½ cups grated onion

1½ cups matzo meal (use flour if not available)

4 eggs

2 teaspoons caraway seeds

Salt and freshly ground pepper

Oil for shallow frying

Remove the meat from the lobsters and cut into pieces. Melt 4 tablespoons (½ stick) of the butter in a skillet and fry the shallots until soft. Add the mushrooms and cook gently until soft, add the lobster, and mix well. Cover and cook very slowly for 3 minutes. Warm the whiskey, set it alight and, when the flames have died down, pour over the lobster. Season with black pepper and cloves and stir in the cream. Shake over the heat until well mixed, cover, and cook over a very low heat for 5 minutes.

To make the latkas, rinse the grated potatoes in several changes of cold water to remove excess starch. Pat dry with a towel and mix with the rest of the ingredients, except the oil. Season well.

Heat enough to shallow fry the latkas in a large skillet. Drop tablespoons of the mixture into the hot oil, flatten each dollop into a round, small flat pancake, and fry over a medium heat for 3–4 minutes on each side until the pancake is a pale golden brown and perfectly crisp. Drain on paper towels and serve very hot with the lobster. If you are being stylish you can stack the latkas with lobster sandwiched between and the sauce drizzled around the base of the stack.

# Crab Boil

George Hirsch                                                    Serves 4

**Crab boil is party food, and you should eat it in clothes that can move right into the washing machine. Ideally, this recipe should be prepared and served out of doors. Old Bay Seasoning can be used, but I like to mix my own ingredients. I put a little beer in with the boil to give it a more pungent flavor. But the most important thing is the crab. You get only about 1 ounce of meat for every crab, so you wind up doing a lot of work and creating a big appetite. Pass around a few crab mallets and fish forks for reaching into the claws for that last piece of meat. Serve with French rolls and lots of ice-cold beer. Although this is called a crab boil, the recipe works just as well with crayfish or shrimp.**

Two 12-ounce bottles beer or strong ale

8 cups cold water

1 cup commercial crab-boil seasoning (or use the following seasoning)

**Seasoning**

¼ cup paprika

1 tablespoon dry mustard

1 tablespoon dried thyme

1 tablespoon dried basil

1 tablespoon dried oregano

1 tablespoon dried parsley

2 tablespoons cayenne

1 tablespoon salt, or to taste

1 teaspoon black pepper

2 onions, chopped

1 cup chopped scallion

1 cup chopped celery

3 whole heads garlic, crushed

3 lemons, halved

¼ cup vegetable oil

24 blue-claw crabs

12 small potatoes

3 ears fresh corn, cut into thirds

Melted butter and lemon wedges

Place a 10- or 12-quart stockpot on the grill and add the beer, water, seasonings, onion, scallion, celery, garlic, lemon halves, and vegetable oil. Bring the mixture to a boil and boil for 20 minutes. The crabs, potatoes, and corn will have to be cooked in several batches; add as many of each as will fit comfortably in the pot. The potatoes and corn will each take about 10 minutes, the crabs from 6 to 8 minutes, depending on their size. Arrange the crabs, potatoes, and corn on platters and pass lemon wedges and bowls of melted butter.

*Grill Temperature: Medium*

# Dragon Well Shrimp

Martin Yan                                                    Serves 4

Tea lends its richly aromatic flavor to dishes throughout eastern China, and shrimp, stir-fried with the tips of Dragon Well green tea leaves, is perhaps the most famous of them all. If Dragon Well tea is unavailable, substitute any high-quality green tea.

**Marinade**

- ½ egg white (1 tablespoon), lightly beaten
- 1 tablespoon cornstarch
- ½ teaspoon salt

- ¾ pound small to medium raw shrimp, shelled and deveined
- ½ cup boiling water
- 1 tablespoon rice wine or dry sherry
- ¾ teaspoon sesame oil
- ⅛ teaspoon white pepper
- 2 tablespoons cooking oil
- 1 teaspoon minced ginger

Combine marinade ingredients in a bowl. Add shrimp and stir to coat. Let stand for 10 minutes.

Combine boiling water and tea leaves in a bowl; let steep for 10 minutes.

Strain ¼ cup of the liquid tea in another bowl and add wine, sesame oil, and pepper. Reserve 1 tablespoon of the rehydrated tea leaves; discard remaining liquid tea and tea leaves.

Place a wok over high heat until hot. Add cooking oil, swirling to coat sides. Add ginger and cook, stirring, until fragrant, about 10 seconds.

Add shrimp and rehydrated tea leaves; stir-fry for 1½ minutes. Add liquid tea mixture and cook until sauce is heated through.

# Daufuskie Island Deviled Crab

Vertamae Grosvenor                                        Serves 8

**Daufuskie cooks hold on to their recipes like misers hold on to their money, so this recipe is from my taste memory of Daufuskie's outstanding culinary accomplishment, deviled crab. On the island, they pack the mixture into crab backs, but little ramekins will do.**

½ small green bell pepper

1 yellow onion

  A few Needa biscuits or plain crackers

1 pound lump crabmeat

1 teaspoon dry mustard

2 tablespoons mayonnaise, or as needed

  Salt, ground black pepper, and cayenne pepper to taste

1 lemon

2 tablespoons butter

Prepare an oven to 350 degrees F.

Seed and chop the bell pepper, and chop the onion. Crush enough biscuits to measure 2 tablespoons.

In a bowl, combine the crabmeat, bell pepper, onion, biscuit crumbs, mustard, and 2 tablespoons mayonnaise. Season with the salt, lots of black pepper, and the cayenne pepper. Stir to mix. Squeeze 1 tablespoon juice from the lemon and add to the bowl. Stir again. If the mixture isn't holding together, add more mayonnaise.

Grease 8 crab backs or an equal number of small ramekins with the butter. Divide crab mixture evenly among them. Bake until heated through and lightly browned, 20 to 30 minutes. Serve hot.

# Seared Scallops with Watercress and Lemon Relish

Joanne Weir                                              Serves 6

**I worked at Chez Panisse for years, and now, every time I go back, I say I am going to give up cooking! The food relies on a few simple principles: The ingredients are of the best quality, the fruits and vegetables full of flavor, and the fish is the freshest it can be. Instead of giving up, I usually just come home and reproduce the dishes with my own spin, which was exactly the inspiration for this dish.**

6 tablespoons extra-virgin olive oil

2 teaspoons grated lemon zest

2 tablespoons chopped fresh flat-leaf parsley

2 shallots, minced

2 tablespoons lemon juice

  Salt and freshly ground black pepper

1½ pounds sea scallops

1 bunch of watercress, stems removed

  Lemon wedges as a garnish

In a small bowl, whisk together 4 tablespoons of the olive oil, the lemon zest, parsley, shallots, and lemon juice. Season to taste with salt and pepper.

Remove the muscle from the side of each scallop and discard. In a large skillet over medium high heat, warm the remaining 2 tablespoons olive oil. Add the scallops in a single layer. Do not overcrowd the pan. Cook the scallops until golden on 1 side, about 2 minutes. Turn the scallops, season with salt and pepper, and continue to cook until the scallops are golden and slightly firm to the touch, 2 to 3 minutes.

To serve, divide the scallops among 6 serving plates. Spoon the relish over the scallops, distributing evenly. Top with the watercress, garnish with lemon wedges, and serve immediately.

# Chesapeake Bay Seafood Stew

John Shields                                                    Serves 8 to 10

**During the eighteenth century, French cuisine was the order of the day in Annapolis, Maryland, which then was considered the cosmopolitan city. Gourmets from all over the new republic made their way to this colonial city to sample the tastes of French fare, including George Washington and Thomas Jefferson. In fact, Jefferson, a devotee of fine cuisine, insisted that all his chefs at his Monticello estate be trained in French cookery in Annapolis. This version of a Chesapeake Bay bouillabaisse, teeming with fresh clams and crabmeat in a saffron-scented tomato broth, is a dish typical of Annapolis. The Rouille, a classic French accompaniment to fish stew, is mayonnaise-like in texture and made from chilies, garlic, and olive oil. Pass around plenty of hot, crusty bread for dipping in the broth.**

¼ cup olive oil

1 large onion, diced

6 cloves garlic, unpeeled

2 leeks, well washed, halved, and cut into pieces

⅓ cup chopped fennel bulb, or 1 tablespoon fennel seed

5 pounds ripe tomatoes, chopped

2 small potatoes, peeled and diced

2 cups dry white wine

3 cups fish stock

1 teaspoon dried thyme leaves

1 teaspoon dried oregano

1 bay leaf

Grated zest of 1 orange

3 or 4 threads of saffron

Salt and freshly ground black pepper, to taste

8 to 10 pieces of French bread, sliced on the diagonal

Melted butter and chopped garlic, for toast

2 pounds bass, rockfish, bluefish, or other firm-fleshed fillets

1 pound backfin crabmeat, picked over

1½ pounds small hard-shell clams, well scrubbed

Rouille (recipe follows)

Chopped parsley

Heat the oil in a heavy pot and sauté the onion, garlic, leeks, and fennel until slightly softened, about 8 to 10 minutes. Add the tomatoes, potatoes, wine, stock, thyme, oregano, and bay leaf. Bring to a boil, reduce the heat, and simmer for 30 minutes.

Puree the mixture in a blender or food processor. Pour through a fine sieve and return to the pot. Add the orange zest, saffron, salt, and pepper. Cook over medium-low heat, stirring frequently, until somewhat reduced, about 20 to 30 minutes.

Meanwhile, preheat the oven to 375°F.

Brush the bread slices with melted butter and top with garlic. Toast in the oven until browned.

Cut the fish in chunks about 2 inches square. Add to the sauce and cook for 8 to 10 minutes, or until the fish is almost done.

Add the crabmeat and clams. Stir, then cover. Cook until the clams have opened. Reserve 1 cup of the liquid for making Rouille.

Prepare the Rouille. Place 1 piece of garlic bread in each bowl, then spoon in the fish and broth. Arrange the clams on top. Garnish with parsley. Serve the Rouille on the side.

# Rouille

1 small potato, peeled

1 cup broth from Chesapeake Bay Seafood Stew

6 cloves garlic

4 fresh or dried red chilies

1 teaspoon Tabasco Sauce

½ cup olive oil

Salt, to taste

Quarter the potato and cook in the reserved broth. Drain, reserving the liquid. Finely chop the garlic and peppers in a blender or a food processor. Add the potato, Tabasco, and oil. Process until the mixture forms a paste. Slowly add enough of the reserved liquid to give the mixture the consistency of mayonnaise. Season with salt.

# Texas Gulf Coast Jambalaya

Stephan Pyles

Serves 4 to 6

**A rustic and complex dish, jambalaya is relatively easy to execute and can be prepared in one dish. It relies on seafood from the Gulf Coast of Texas and Mexico, but can be prepared with whatever fish is available to you. After all, jambalaya is merely a variation on the classic Spanish dish, paella.**

¼ cup olive oil

¾ cup chorizo sausage (about 6 ounces)

⅔ cup tasso ham

2 cups finely chopped onion

6 scallions, chopped

6 garlic cloves, minced

1 large green bell pepper, seeded and finely chopped

1 large red bell pepper, seeded and finely chopped

6 stalks celery, finely chopped

8 ripe tomatoes (about 2 pounds), blanched, peeled, seeded and chopped

1 tablespoon chopped fresh oregano

2 teaspoons chopped fresh basil

1 tablespoon chopped fresh cilantro

1 teaspoon chopped fresh thyme

3 bay leaves

1 teaspoon ground cumin

2 teaspoons cayenne powder

3 cups chicken stock

3 cups uncooked rice

24 medium size raw shrimp, peeled and deveined

24 fresh Gulf Coast oysters (about 1 pound), shucked and in their liquor

8 ounces fresh Gulf Coast crabmeat, shell and cartilage removed

Salt to taste

Preheat oven to 350°F.

Heat the olive oil in a large, oven-proof saucepan or casserole until lightly smoking. Add the chorizo and tasso, and sauté over medium heat until crisp, 6 to 8 minutes. Add the onion, scallions, garlic, bell peppers, and celery, and sauté for 5 minutes more.

Add the tomatoes and seasonings, stir thoroughly, and cook for 5 minutes. Stir in the stock and bring to a boil. Add the rice; stir well. Remove from the heat. Cover the pan with foil, place in the oven, and bake until the rice is just tender, about 15 minutes.

Stir in the shrimp, oysters, and crabmeat. Cover and bake for 15 minutes more. Remove the bay leaves. Season with salt to taste and serve immediately.

# Main Courses— Meat and Poultry

## WITH JACQUES PÉPIN

Jacques Pépin was to the kitchen born. As a child he worked in his parents' restaurant outside the French culinary mecca of Lyons; at age thirteen he began an apprenticeship at the Grand Hôtel de l'Europe. By the time Jacques left for America in 1959, he had worked in acclaimed Parisian restaurants and served as personal chef to three French heads of state. On this side of the Atlantic, he cooked at New York's famed Le Pavillon and is now dean of studies at the French Culinary Institute in Manhattan.

Many a chef-in-training knows Jacques from his classic works *La Technique* and *La Méthode*, and many a public television viewer has been seduced into carving tomato roses and whipping up meringues after watching Jacques' easy elegance with a knife and whisk on his *Cooking Techniques* programs. In his *Today's Gourmet* series, he lightened classic dishes to suit '90s sensibilities, and in his cooking shows with daughter Claudine he has introduced a new generation to the basics. His latest, *Julia and Jacques: Cooking at Home*, with Julia Child, is a meeting of the masters. As with every recipe Jacques creates, his dishes in this chapter and throughout the book teach you skills you'll be able to apply to countless other preparations.

# Tournedos of Beef Du Barry

Jacques Pépin                                                                                      Serves 6

**In classic French cooking, dishes were often named after famous people, usually a member of the nobility prior to the nineteenth century. The Countess Du Barry, a favorite of Louis XV who ended up on the guillotine during the French revolution, has the gastronomic distinction of having her name associated with cauliflower. Any dish, from a soup to a fish to our tournedos, containing the name "Du Barry" has a garnish of cauliflower. In this recipe, cauliflower florets are used as a "cushion" under sautéed tournedos. Tournedos are beef steaks cut from the center of a beef fillet or tenderloin.  Small, round, and a good 1 1/4 inches thick, they are usually sautéed or grilled.  Here, the meat is finished with a Madeira sauce and tarragon. I prefer the Bual type of Madeira to the very sweet Malmsey and very dry Sercial. In addition to the cauliflower garnish, the tournedos are served with potato *miettes* (crumb in French), small pieces of potato that are fried in a skillet.  Although the cauliflower and tournedos are served together here, I have created separate recipes for these dishes, but they can also be served on their own in other menu combinations.**

1 center piece beef fillet partially trimmed at the market (about 3 pounds)

4 tablespoons unsalted butter

½ teaspoon salt, plus additional as needed

½ teaspoon freshly ground black pepper, plus additional as needed

½ cup Madeira, preferably Bual

⅓ cup tomato sauce (canned is fine)

⅓ cup water

1 tablespoon Worcestershire sauce

1½ tablespoons chopped fresh tarragon

Preheat the oven to 180 degrees.

Remove all surrounding fat, the silver skin and the "chain" (the long sinewy strip) from the piece of beef. It should be completely clean and weigh about 2¼ pounds. Cut the beef into 6 tournedos, each weighing 5 to 6 ounces and measuring about 1¼ inches thick.

At serving time, heat 2 tablespoons of the butter in a large skillet, preferably one made of thick copper or aluminum. Sprinkle the tournedos on both sides with ½ teaspoon salt and ½ teaspoon pepper. When the butter is very hot and beginning to smoke, place the tournedos in the skillet and cook them over high heat for about 2 minutes on each side. Transfer the tournedos into a large ovenproof platter and keep them warm in the 180-degree oven while you complete the recipe.

Add the Madeira to the drippings in the skillet and cook for about 30 seconds.  Stir in the tomato sauce, water, and Worcestershire sauce and cook over high heat for about 1 minute longer.  Remove the skillet from the heat. Add the remaining 2 tablespoons of butter and the tarragon and stir well to mix them into the sauce.  Add additional salt and pepper if needed.

To serve, arrange 3 cauliflower florets (Sautéed Cauliflower Florets recipe follows) in the shape of an open flower with the stems in the center of each of six warm plates. Place a tournedo on top of the cauliflower on each plate and spoon some sauce on the top and around them. Serve immediately with Potato *Miettes* (recipe follows).

# Sautéed Cauliflower Florets

Serves 6

1 head cauliflower (about 2¼ pounds) with all green leaves and central core removed (about 2 pounds trimmed weight)

3 tablespoons canola oil

1 tablespoon unsalted butter

¼ teaspoon salt

Preheat the oven to 180 degrees.

Heat 2 cups of water in a deep saucepan until it comes to a boil. Place the whole, trimmed cauliflower head stem side down in the water, and bring the water back to a boil. Cover and boil over high heat for about 10 minutes or until the cauliflower is tender, but still firm when pierced with the sharp point of a knife. Transfer the cauliflower to a plate and let it cool to lukewarm.

Divide the cauliflower into about 10 large florets then cut the florets in half lengthwise to have about 20 pieces, each with one flat side.

Divide the oil and butter between two skillets, preferably nonstick, and heat. Arrange the florets flat side down in one layer in the hot skillets and sprinkle them with the salt.

Sauté the florets over medium to high heat for 8 to 10 minutes, turning them after 4 or 5 minutes so they are nicely brown on both sides. Place in the 180 degree oven to keep hot until serving time.

# Potato *Miettes*

Serves 6

2¼ pounds baking potatoes (about 5)

¼ cup canola oil

½ teaspoon salt

¼ teaspoon freshly ground black pepper

1 tablespoon chopped fresh chives

1 tablespoon unsalted butter

Peel the potatoes and cut them lengthwise into pieces about ¾-inch thick. Stack the slices and cut lengthwise to form ¾-inch sticks. Cut the sticks crosswise into thin pieces, ⅛–¼ inch thick (you should have about 6 cups). Place the potatoes in cold water to cover.

When ready to cook, heat the oil in a large 12-inch nonstick skillet. Drain the potatoes and rinse them well under cold water. Place them on paper towels and pat them gently to remove some of the water.

Add the potato *miettes* to the hot oil, and cook them over high heat, tossing occasionally for 20 to 25 minutes, or until they are nicely brown and crisp on both sides. Add the salt, pepper, chives, and butter. Toss briefly and serve.

# Hamburger Brennan

Brennan's Executive Chef Michael Roussel

Serves 6

2 pounds ground chuck

¼ cup minced scallions

¼ cup minced onion

2 tablespoons Worcestershire sauce

1 tablespoon chopped fresh parsley

2 large eggs

Pinch of nutmeg

1½ teaspoons salt

½ teaspoon black pepper

1½ cups Sauce Maison (recipe follows)

Preheat a grill or broiler.

Combine all of the ingredients in a large bowl. When the mixture is well combined, shape into 6 oval patties. Grill or broil the patties until cooked according to your preference; reserve 1 cup cooking juices for preparation of the accompanying sauce. Drizzle sauce maison on each patty and serve.

## Sauce Maison

Makes 1½ cups

¾ cup (1½ sticks) butter

2 tablespoons Worcestershire sauce

1 cup meat juices (beef stock can be substituted)

1 teaspoon chopped fresh parsley

In a small skillet, cook the butter over medium heat until golden brown. Stir in the Worcestershire and meat juices and cook for 1 minute. Add the parsley and keep the sauce warm until serving.

# Grilled Seven-Bone Steak

George Hirsch                                               Serves 4

**Seven-bone steak, or chuck steak, is one of the most economical of all beef steaks and one of the tastiest. The marinade doesn't really tenderize the steak, but it does enhance the flavor. Trim the fat to about 1/4 inch and make small cuts in the fat with a sharp knife to prevent the steak from curling up on the grill.**

6 cloves garlic, sliced

2 teaspoons Tabasco sauce

2 teaspoons soy sauce

2 teaspoons freshly ground black pepper

2 tablespoons olive oil

2 seven-bone blade steaks or cross-cut chuck steaks, about 1½ pounds each with bone

1 recipe Olive Relish (recipe follows)

Combine the garlic, Tabasco, soy sauce, pepper, and olive oil in a small bowl. Rub the mixture onto both sides of the steaks, and marinate for an hour or two in the refrigerator. Place the steaks on a hot grill for 1 minute. Using tongs, turn the steaks 45 degrees to make a crosshatch mark. Cook for 2 to 3 minutes more, and turn the steaks over. Move the steaks to a cooler edge of the grill, or raise the cooking grid, or lower the heat to medium, and cook until done. Avoid turning the steaks from side to side.

*Grill Temperature: High, then medium.*

# Olive Relish

Serves 4

½ cup green olives, pitted and chopped

½ cup plum tomatoes, seeded and chopped

1 tablespoon chopped fresh basil

2 to 4 jalapeño peppers, seeded and chopped

Juice of 1 lemon

Salt and pepper to taste

In a small bowl, combine all of the ingredients and mix well.

# Triple Pepper Steak

## Martin Yan

**Attention beef lovers. This one is for you! Wok-seared slices of tender steak in a robust brown sauce, with a colorful medley of sweet bell peppers.**

1 pound flank steak, thinly sliced diagonally

### Marinade

2 tablespoons oyster flavored sauce

2 teaspoons cornstarch

½ teaspoon black pepper

½ each green, red, and yellow bell pepper, julienned

### Sauce

⅓ cup beef broth

2 tablespoons rice wine or dry sherry

2 tablespoons dark soy sauce

1 teaspoon cornstarch

1 teaspoon sugar

½ teaspoon black pepper

3 tablespoons cooking oil

2 tablespoons water

1 teaspoon minced garlic

½ teaspoon minced ginger

Jalapeño or serrano chili slices for garnish

Combine marinade ingredients in a bowl. Add beef and stir to coat. Let stand for 10 minutes. Combine sauce ingredients in a bowl; set aside.

Place a wok over high heat until hot. Add 1 tablespoon oil, swirling to coat sides. Add bell peppers and stir-fry for 1 minute. Add water and stir-fry until bell peppers are crisp-tender, 2 to 3 minutes. Remove bell peppers to a serving plate.

Add remaining 2 tablespoons oil to wok, swirling to coat sides. Add beef and pan-fry until browned on both sides, but pink within, 1½ to 2 minutes on each side. Remove the beef from the wok.

Remove all but ½ teaspoon oil from wok. Add garlic and ginger; stir-fry until fragrant, about 10 seconds. Return beef to wok and add sauce; cook until sauce boils and thickens. Place beef over bell peppers and garnish with chili slices.

# Flank Steak with Crispy Polenta and Roasted Shallot Vinaigrette

Charlie Trotter
Serves 4

**Once the polenta is made (which, for convenience, can be done a day or two ahead of time) this dish is a snap to put together. Simply sauté the polenta pieces, grill the flank steak, place them on the plate, and spoon on the luscious roasted shallot vinaigrette and you have a quick and very satisfying plate of food. A mound of sautéed mushrooms, or for something lighter, asparagus or haricots verts, is a perfect accompaniment. Crispy potatoes are a splendid substitute for the polenta.**

4 shallots, peeled

1 cup olive oil

3 tablespoons balsamic vinegar

2 tablespoons chopped fresh chives

Salt and pepper

2 tablespoons chopped garlic

¼ cup butter

2 cups cooked polenta, hot

4 4-ounce pieces flank steak

10 sprigs thyme

**Method**

To prepare the vinaigrette: Place the shallots and ¾ cup of the olive oil in a small ovenproof pan and cover tightly. Bake at 350 degrees for 50 to 60 minutes, or until the shallots are soft. Let the shallots cool in the olive oil, and then remove, reserving the oil. Julienne the shallots and put them in a bowl. Add the balsamic vinegar and slowly whisk in the reserved olive oil. Add the chopped chives and season to taste with salt and pepper.

To prepare the polenta: Cook the garlic in 3 tablespoons of butter for 1 minute. Fold into the polenta and season to taste with salt and pepper. Spread the polenta into a ½-inch-thick layer on a small sheet pan. Cover with plastic wrap and refrigerate for 2 hours. Cut the polenta into four 3-inch discs and sauté in the remaining 1 tablespoon butter in a hot, nonstick pan for 2 to 3 minutes on each side, or until golden brown and crispy. Blot on paper towels.

To prepare the steak: Season the steak with salt and pepper and rub with ¼ cup olive oil. Remove the thyme leaves from the stems and rub them onto the beef. Grill for 5 to 7 minutes on each side, or until medium-rare.

**Assembly**

Place a piece of the polenta in the center of each plate and top with a piece of the steak. Spoon the Roasted Shallot Vinaigrette over the steak and around the plates and top with freshly ground black pepper.

*Wine Notes: The warm garlic flavors in the polenta mesh beautifully with Italian varietals. The rich fruit of Barbera d'Alba from a producer like Giacomo Conterno beautifully balances the garlic, and has the full acidity needed for the shallot vinaigrette.*

# Tangy Peach Short Ribs of Beef

John Shields                                     Serves 3 to 4

**These ribs, braised in a lightly sweetened stock with spiced peaches, are so tender the meat falls from the bone. As the braising juices cook down during the baking, they thicken into a sweet, tasty sauce that's finger-licking good.**

3 pounds beef short ribs, cut into 3-inch pieces

All-purpose flour seasoned with salt, freshly ground black pepper, and cayenne

¼ cup vegetable oil or rendered beef fat

1 onion, finely diced

2 cloves garlic, minced

¾ cup beef stock

2 cups peeled and sliced peaches

3 tablespoons dark brown sugar

3 tablespoons cider vinegar

½ teaspoon ground cinnamon

¼ teaspoon ground cloves

Preheat the oven to 325°F.

Dust the ribs with the seasoned flour. Heat the oil in a dutch oven and brown the ribs well on all sides. Remove the ribs and set aside. Pour off all but 3 tablespoons of the fat from the pot. Add the onion and garlic to the pot and sauté briefly. Return the ribs to the pot and add all the remaining ingredients. Mix well, bring to a boil, and cover the pot.

Place the pot in the oven and bake for 1½ to 2 hours, basting the ribs often. When done, remove the ribs and cut into serving pieces. Let the sauce stand for several minutes and degrease. Pour a small amount of sauce over the ribs and serve remaining sauce on the side.

# Beef and Bell Pepper Stew

Nick Stellino                                    Serves 4 to 5

**The beef in this colorful stew cooks until it becomes fork-tender, while the peppers provide a mysterious subtle sweetness.**

1½ pounds cubed beef stew meat

¾ teaspoon salt

½ teaspoon black pepper

1½ tablespoons flour

4 tablespoons olive oil

4 garlic cloves, thickly sliced

¼ teaspoon red pepper flakes

3 large bell peppers, preferably 1 each red, yellow and green, cut into 1½-inch pieces

1 onion, cut into 1½-inch pieces

2 teaspoons thyme

2 bay leaves

1 cup dry red wine

3 cups beef stock

2 cups Tomato Sauce (recipe follows)

2 tablespoons chopped fresh Italian parsley

Sprinkle the meat cubes with the salt, pepper and flour, shaking off any excess. Heat 3 tablespoons of the olive oil in a Dutch oven set on high heat until sizzling, about 2 minutes. Add the meat in a single layer, being careful not to crowd the meat pieces—cook in 2 batches, if necessary. Cook the meat until well-browned on all sides, about 3–4 minutes. Transfer the meat to a plate or bowl with a slotted spoon. Set aside.

Add the remaining oil to the same pan set on high heat. Add the garlic, red pepper flakes, bell peppers, onion, thyme, and bay leaves. Cook until the peppers are beginning to soften and the onion is translucent, about 4–5 minutes. Return the browned meat to the pan along with

any juices that have accumulated. Stir in the wine and boil until reduced by half, about 4 minutes. Add the beef stock and tomato sauce and bring to a boil. Reduce the heat to low and simmer, with the lid slightly ajar, for 1 hour. Remove the lid and cook 30 minutes longer. Stir in the parsley and the stew is ready to serve.

*Cook's Tip: To add a sweet-and-sour dimension to the stew, boil 1 tablespoon sugar and 2 tablespoons balsamic vinegar in a small saucepan set on high heat until reduced by half and quite syrupy, about 2 minutes. Stir the syrup and 1 teaspoon cocoa powder into the finished stew and cook for 2 minutes.*

*Wine Suggestion: Merlot*

## Tomato Sauce                    Makes 5¾ cups

4 tablespoons olive oil

4 whole garlic cloves

¾ cup finely chopped onions

2 (28-ounce) cans peeled Italian tomatoes

10 fresh basil leaves or 1 teaspoon dried

Pour the olive oil into a 3-quart saucepan set on medium-high heat and cook garlic and onion for 3–5 minutes. Reduce the heat to a simmer and cook until the onions are soft and begin to brown, about 10 minutes, stirring occasionally.

While the onions are cooking, put the tomatoes and their juices in a food processor or blender and process until smooth. Add the tomato purée to the onion mixture, raise the heat to high and bring to a

boil for 5–8 minutes. Reduce the heat, add the basil and simmer for 25 minutes, stirring occasionally.

*Cook's Tip: I can't stress enough the importance of using Italian tomatoes because they're naturally sweeter. If you have to use American tomatoes, double the amount of chopped onions and add 2 tablespoons of olive oil. Remember, this is a plain, unsalted sauce, which is great as an ingredient in other finished sauces. If you want to use this as a garnish for your pasta, I'd suggest you add ¼ teaspoon of salt for each 2 cups, according to your taste.*

# Stuffed Cabbage with Cranberry Sauce

Joan Nathan

Makes at least 15 stuffed
cabbages or 6 to 8 servings

**The following stuffed cabbage with cranberries comes from Massachusetts.**

1 16-ounce can jellied
cranberry sauce

1 15- or 16-ounce can
tomato sauce

1½ cups water

Juice of 1 lemon

¼ cup brown sugar or to taste

½ cup raisins

½ cup fresh cranberries

1 apple

1 medium head of cabbage

2 pounds ground beef

½ cup uncooked rice

Salt and freshly ground pepper

1 large egg

1 medium onion, grated

4 tablespoons ketchup

Mix the cranberry sauce, tomato sauce, 1 cup water, lemon, and sugar in a saucepan. Bring to a boil; then add the raisins and the fresh cranberries. Peel, core, and dice the apple and add. Simmer for another 5 minutes.

Core the cabbage and place in a large pot with water to cover. Bring to a boil and then simmer, covered, about 10 minutes or until wilted. Cover with cold water and drain. (Alternately, you can place the cored cabbage in the freezer for several days. Defrost 24 hours before making the cabbage. It will wilt naturally.)

In a large bowl mix the meat, rice, salt and freshly ground pepper to taste, egg, onion, ½ cup water, and ketchup, blending with your fingers until well mixed.

Trim the ribs off the cabbage, remove the outside leaves, and line a large flameproof casserole with them. Pull off the inside leaves and place them one by one on a board, outside down. Fill with a heaping tablespoon or two of the filling, depending on the size of the leaf. Fold up like an envelope, top first, then bottom and then the 2 sides. Place seam side down in the lined casserole. Repeat with the rest of the cabbage and the filling.

Pour the sauce over the stuffed cabbage and simmer, covered, for 2 hours. Then place the stuffed cabbage in a preheated 300-degree oven and bake, uncovered, for one half hour more.

*Tip: Another American way to make this dish is to make a sauce of ¾ cup ketchup, 1½ to 2 cups tomato juice, ¾ cup brown sugar, the juice of 1 large lemon, and sour salt to taste. Make this dish ahead. It tastes much better the next day. Also, this is a good recipe to double. Freeze one portion for unexpected guests.*

# Braised Lamb Shanks with Roasted Shallots and Dried Cherries

Caprial Pence — Serves 6

**We serve lamb shanks often in the fall and winter at the restaurant and also prepare them in our cooking classes. Lamb shanks tend to be very tough because they are from a part of the animal that gets a lot of exercise. Braising the meat with acidic substances like vinegar and wine breaks down that toughness and allows the best flavor to come through. Look for dried cherries at gourmet markets. I like to serve the shanks over couscous.**

2 tablespoons olive oil

8 shallots, peeled

6 whole cloves garlic

6 (10- to 12-ounce) lamb shanks

Salt

Freshly ground black pepper

½ cup all-purpose flour

1 cup red wine

2½ cups lamb or veal stock

3 tablespoons balsamic vinegar

1 cup dried cherries

1 tablespoon chopped fresh thyme

Preheat oven to 300°. Put the olive oil, shallots, and garlic in a large roasting pan, cover with a lid, and place in the oven. Roast for about 1 hour, or until the shallots and garlic are soft to the touch. Remove the pan from the oven and place on the stovetop over high heat. Season the shanks with salt and pepper. Place the flour on a large plate and dredge the lamb in it. Place the shanks in the pan and sear both sides well, about 2 minutes on each side.

Add the wine and reduce over high heat by about half. Add the stock, vinegar, cherries, and thyme, cover with a lid, and place in the oven. Cook until tender, 1 to 1½ hours. Remove the pan from the oven and season the broth to taste with the salt and pepper. Place the lamb on a serving platter. Slice and serve hot with the sauce spooned over.

# Lamb Couscous with Tomatoes

Lynn Fischer                                     Serves 6

**This Moroccan specialty is a meal in itself. A flavorful mix of vegetables, spices, and lamb sits atop the couscous, tiny granules of semolina flour. Although it is a grain, couscous cooks in minutes and is a type of pasta; rice can be substituted for the couscous. Find it in most supermarkets or in Middle Eastern markets. Although lamb makes the dish authentic, you may substitute 3 ounces of cooked chicken or turkey.**

2 cups couscous, cooked according to package directions, or rice

1 cup water or low-sodium, defatted chicken stock

1 onion, coarsely chopped

3 cloves garlic, minced

1 carrot, diced

1½ cups shredded cabbage

¼ teaspoon freshly ground black pepper

Pinch cayenne pepper or Cajun spice

Large pinch powdered saffron

**Lamb**

Olive oil spray

½ pound very lean lamb, diced

½ teaspoon Worcestershire

½ teaspoon garlic powder

½ cup currants or raisins

½ cup garbanzo beans (chickpeas), drained

½ teaspoon ground turmeric

1 teaspoon freshly grated ginger

3 tablespoon chopped parsley

4 medium tomatoes, parboiled, skins and stems removed, and cut into 1½-inch cubes

2 tablespoons harissa, ½ teaspoon Tabasco, or hot sauce

If the couscous is cold, place it in a small saucepan over medium heat to warm; set aside.

In a large nonstick skillet over medium-high heat, heat the water; add the onion, garlic, carrot, cabbage, pepper, cayenne, and saffron and cook, stirring occasionally, and adding more liquid if the mixture becomes too dry, for about 7 minutes, or until the vegetables are nearly tender.

Meanwhile, in a small nonstick skillet lightly sprayed with olive oil, over high heat, cook the lamb, Worcestershire, and garlic powder until the meat is well browned. Remove from the heat, and cover loosely with foil.

To the large skillet, add the currants, garbanzo beans, turmeric, ginger, and parsley and cook 2 to 3 minutes. Add the couscous to the skillet and heat thoroughly. Mound the couscous mixture on individual plates and top with the diced tomatoes and lamb. Serve with harissa.

# Rack of Lamb Côte d'Azur-style
## *Carré d'Agneau Côte d'Azur*

Pierre Franey                                                      Serves 4

---

3 tablespoons olive oil

4 tablespoons dried bread crumbs, pressed through a fine sieve

1 tablespoon shallots, finely chopped

1 teaspoon garlic, finely chopped

1 teaspoon parsley, finely chopped

Salt and freshly ground pepper to taste

2 racks of lamb, well trimmed of the fat and skin

2 sprigs fresh rosemary, or ¼ teaspoon dried

2 sprigs fresh thyme, or ¼ teaspoon dried

4 sprigs fresh thyme or rosemary, for garnish

Vegetable garnish (recipe follows)

Prepare outdoor charcoal grill (with a lid) to high heat.

In a small mixing bowl, combine 1 tablespoon of the olive oil, the dried bread crumbs, shallots, garlic, parsley, and salt and pepper to taste. Mix well.

Sprinkle the racks of lamb with salt and pepper and brush them with 1 tablespoon olive oil. Be sure to brush especially well on the meat side.

Place the lamb on the hot grill, meat side down, about 4 inches from the coals. Sprinkle with rosemary and thyme. Cook until lightly browned, then turn and cook on second side (about 5 minutes total).

Transfer the lamb to an ovenproof dish and sprinkle both sides of each rack with equal amounts of the bread crumb mixture and the remaining olive oil. With the barbecue lid shut, roast the lamb for about 12 to 15 minutes more, basting from time to time with the cooking juices.

Remove the lamb from the grill and let sit in its dish in a warm place for about 5 minutes before slicing. Leaving the racks in the dish, slice them into two-chop sections. The juices will blend with the bread crumbs. Place 2 pieces on each of 4 warmed serving plates and spoon the cooking juices over the meat after removing the herb sprigs. Spoon vegetable garnish (recipe follows) beside the lamb and garnish each plate with a sprig of fresh thyme or rosemary.

# Sautéed Julienne Vegetables
## *Sauté de Julienne de Légumes*

Serves 4

---

1 cup carrots, peeled and trimmed

1 cup white turnips, trimmed

1½ cups zucchini, trimmed

1 tablespoon olive oil

½ tablespoon garlic, finely chopped

1 tablespoon parsley, finely chopped

Salt and freshly ground pepper to taste

Using a mandoline or a vegetable slicer, shred the carrots, turnips, and zucchini.

In a large nonstick skillet, heat the olive oil over medium heat and add the carrots. Cook, stirring, for about 2 minutes.

Add the turnips and continue to cook for 1–2 minutes. Add the zucchini and garlic and toss the vegetables together. Continue to cook until tender but still slightly crisp. The total cooking time should be about 5 minutes.

Sprinkle with parsley and salt and pepper to taste.

# Grilled Pork Medallions with Watercress Salad

Roy Yamaguchi                                                 Serves 4

**For crispier shoestring potatoes, first soak them in water to remove the starch. Rinse them well, and dry them thoroughly before frying.**

## Pork

- 1 quart warm water
- 1 green bell pepper, chopped
- ½ onion, chopped
- 2 bay leaves
- 10 peppercorns
- ½ cup sugar
- 4 (7-ounce) pork chops, or 2 pork tenderloins

## Watercress Bed

- 2 tablespoons sesame oil
- ½ teaspoon minced ginger
- ½ teaspoon minced garlic
- 2 cups fresh shiitake mushrooms, sliced
- ½ cup watercress stems
- 1 cup red bell peppers, sliced in thin strips
- 2 cups bean sprouts
- ½ tablespoon oyster sauce
- 1 teaspoon white sesame seeds

## Shoestring Potatoes

- 1 potato, julienned
- 1 pint oil for frying

## Watercress Salad

- 3 tablespoons olive oil
- ⅛ teaspoon minced ginger
- ⅛ teaspoon minced garlic
- ½ teaspoon chili paste
- 3 tablespoons rice wine vinegar, or any delicate vinegar
- 10 cups (½ pound) watercress leaves, top 2 inches
- 2 to 4 tablespoons roasted, crushed Hawaiian macadamia nuts

### Preparation of the pork

Combine all the ingredients in a large bowl and marinate the pork overnight.

Grill the pork to desired doneness. Slice it into ⅛-inch-thick medallions, and set it aside.

### Preparation of the watercress bed

Heat the sesame oil in a medium sauté pan. Sauté the ginger, garlic, mushrooms, watercress stems and bell peppers over medium heat for 1 minute.

Add the bean sprouts and oyster sauce. Sauté the mixture for another 30 seconds, and sprinkle in the sesame seeds. Set the mixture aside.

### Preparation of the shoestring potatoes

Soak the thin potato slivers in water for 1 hour.

Drain and rinse the potato well, then pat dry.

In a fryer or large saucepan, fry the potato in the oil for 1½ to 2 minutes, until the slivers are crispy and golden brown.

Place the potato on a piece of paper towel to drain the excess oil.

Reserve a handful of shoestring pieces for garnish.

### Preparation of the watercress salad

Heat the olive oil in a large pan, and sauté the ginger and garlic for 15 seconds. Add the chili paste and vinegar.

Remove the mixture from the heat, and place it in a large salad bowl. Add the watercress and macadamia nuts, and toss with the shoestring potatoes.

# Spice-Rubbed Pork Tenderloin in Corn Husks

Barbara Pool Fenzl                                    Serves 6

**Corn husks are a terrific wrapper for tamales, but also for many other fillings. They keep the filling moist, impart a wonderful corn flavor, and make a lovely presentation. This is the perfect entertaining dish. It requires just 20 minutes in the oven and can cook while your guests finish their soup.**

### Southwest Spice Rub

- 2 teaspoons cumin seed
- 2 teaspoons whole coriander seed
- 2 tablespoons chile powder
- 2 teaspoons sugar
- 1 teaspoon salt
- 1 teaspoon black peppercorns
- ½ teaspoon cayenne pepper

- 1½ pounds pork tenderloin, trimmed and cut into 6 equal pieces
- 9 dried corn husks, soaked in warm water until soft, about 1 hour, cleaned, and patted dry
   Dried Cherry Salsa (see page 61), for accompaniment

### For the spice rub

Place the cumin seed in a small dry skillet over medium-high heat and toast until lightly browned and aromatic. Transfer into a mini food processor, coffee grinder, or spice grinder and puree. Toast the coriander in the same skillet and add to the cumin in the grinder. Puree again. Add the remaining ingredients and puree until well blended. Turn out onto a plate.

Preheat an oven to 375°.

Roll each piece of pork in the spice mix and place in the center of a corn husk. Tear 3 corn husks into strips. Wrap the corn husk around the pork and tie each end with a corn husk strip. Repeat with the remaining pieces of pork and corn husks. Place the pork packages on a baking sheet and bake until a meat thermometer registers 145°, 25 to 30 minutes.

To serve, place one package on each plate and remove the corn husk strip from one end. Fold the corn husk back to expose the meat. Serve with dried cherry salsa.

*Do Ahead: The spice mix can be made months ahead, and the pork packages themselves can be assembled a day ahead if covered with a damp towel (so the corn husks don't dry out) and refrigerated. The dried cherry salsa can be made a day ahead without the cilantro; add the cilantro just before serving.*

*Tip: Make more of the rub than you need for this recipe, and keep the extra stored airtight in the pantry. It's also a great gift, especially for someone who doesn't live in the Southwest, but craves the flavors.*

# Orange-Glazed Baked Ham with Rosemary

Marcia Adams — Serves 12, with leftovers

**Hams are considered a special treat among the Amish and are reserved for important occasions. A whole or half a ham would be served to the immediate family for a birthday dinner or Easter meal; for a large group, a creative Amish cook might make a ham loaf or ham balls, which extends the costly ham a lot further. I find the Mennonites serve ham more frequently than the Amish. The hams available in our supermarkets today are generally cooked during their processing, have the rind and bones removed, and need only to be heated to 140°F. to set the glaze. If the ham has a rind, leave that on throughout most of the cooking time to baste the meat. Cut off the rind for the last 1/2 to 1 hour of baking, then stud the ham with cloves and add the glaze. If the meat has no rind, you can stud it with cloves at the beginning of the baking.**

1 boneless ham half (approximately 4 pounds)

30 whole cloves

¼ cup orange marmalade or apricot jam

½ cup dark brown sugar, packed

2 tablespoons prepared horseradish mustard

2 teaspoons fresh rosemary leaves, or 1 teaspoon dried, crumbled.

Preheat the oven to 325°F. Line a 9x13-inch dish with foil, add a baking rack, and place the ham on the rack. Insert the whole cloves into the ham and bake for 1½ hours, or until the meat thermometer registers 130°F.

Meanwhile, in a 2-cup measure, combine the marmalade, brown sugar, mustard, and rosemary. Microwave on high for 3 minutes.

Drizzle the sauce over the ham and bake ½ hour longer or until the ham registers 140°F. and the outside of the ham is crusty and sugary brown. Baste occasionally. Remove from the oven and allow the ham to stand for 10 minutes before carving.

Slice thinly (an electric knife is ideal for this) and serve hot or cold.

# Duck in Red Wine Sauce

Jennifer Paterson and Clarissa Dickson Wright, Two Fat Ladies

**This is a useful dish to prepare in advance if you are a working person. Just heat it up before you need to eat it. As with many a casserole dish, the flavors intensify on reheating. JP**

4-pound duck, cut into serving pieces

Salt and freshly ground pepper

2 tablespoons all-purpose flour

4 tablespoons (½ stick) butter

2 tablespoons olive oil

½ cup chopped shallots

4 ounces bacon, cut into narrow strips (lardons)

1¼ cups red wine

6 crushed black peppercorns

1 bay leaf

2½ cups chicken stock

16 whole pearl onions

1 teaspoon sugar

3 cups sliced mushrooms

**For the Beurre Manié**

3 tablespoons (¼ stick) butter, softened

2½ tablespoons all-purpose flour

Sprinkle the duck pieces with salt, pepper, and flour. Melt 2 tablespoons of the butter and 1 tablespoon of oil in a large skillet and sauté the duck pieces until golden brown. Place the duck pieces in a casserole. Cook the shallots and bacon in the oil and butter in the skillet for a few minutes. Add the wine, peppercorns, and bay leaf. Bring to a boil to reduce by half, then add the stock and again reduce by half. Strain the sauce over the duck and cook gently in a pre-heated 375°F oven for 1 hour, but check to make sure the duck pieces are cooked.

Meanwhile, melt the remaining butter and oil in the skillet. Add the onions, sprinkle with sugar, and fry until brown. After the duck has been cooking for 30 minutes, add the onions and the mushrooms.

When the duck pieces are cooked, set them aside. Check the sauce for consistency and seasoning and, if necessary, thicken with the beurre manié. To make this, knead the butter and flour together and form into a small knob.

# Tamarind-Glazed Roasted Chicken with Apple-Onion-Potato Purée

Charlie Trotter                                         Serves 4

**The tamarind glaze provides a refreshing, sweet-sour tanginess that perfectly highlights the succulent roasted chicken. The apple-onion-potato purée acts as an elegant, satiny bed for the chicken pieces. This is a great dish for the cool evenings of fall. Braised celery or leeks would make a great accompanying vegetable for this preparation.**

2 cups freshly squeezed orange juice

½ cup seedless tamarind paste

1 3- to 4-pound chicken, trussed

Salt and pepper

1 cup julienned Spanish onions

3½ tablespoons butter

1 Idaho potato, peeled, diced, and boiled

1 McIntosh apple, peeled, cored, and chopped

½ cup chicken stock

¼ cup heavy cream

1 McIntosh apple, thinly sliced

4 winter savory sprigs

4 baby thyme sprigs

**Method**

To make the tamarind glaze: Whisk the orange juice and tamarind paste over medium heat for 5 minutes, or until smooth.

To cook the chicken: Place the trussed chicken in a roasting pan and season with salt and pepper. Brush the chicken all over with the tamarind glaze and roast at 325 degrees for 60 to 90 minutes, or until the juices run clear. Brush on additional glaze every 15 minutes during the roasting. Cover the legs of the chicken with aluminum foil if they become too dark during roasting. Bring the remaining tamarind glaze to a boil. Reduce to a simmer and cook for 5 minutes.

To make the purée: Cook the onions with ½ tablespoon of the butter over medium heat for 10 minutes, or until golden brown and caramelized. Remove two thirds of the onions and reserve them for garnish. Add the potato, chopped apple, and stock to the pan and simmer for 7 to 8 minutes, or until the apple is tender.

Purée the mixture in a food processor with 2 tablespoons of butter and the cream until smooth. Season to taste with salt and pepper.

To prepare the apples: Sauté the apple slices in the remaining 1 tablespoon of butter over medium heat for 5 minutes, or until tender.

**Assembly**

Carve the chicken. Arrange some of the reserved caramelized onions, the apple slices, and roasted chicken in the center of each plate. Spoon a ring of the purée around the chicken and spoon the tamarind glaze over the chicken and around the plate. Garnish with the reserved onion, savory, and thyme sprigs and top with freshly ground black pepper.

*Wine Notes: The rich fruit of an American Pinot Blanc is the perfect balance for the apple and caramelized onion in the potato purée. Etude from Carneros has rich fruit and a fair amount of oak that will wonderfully complement the tamarind on the chicken.*

# Two-Hour Turkey and Gravy

Nathalie Dupree

Serves 10 to 12

**The trick to having a turkey ready in two hours is to use a hot oven and a small turkey. I learned this recipe originally from Julia Child, but I've changed it along the way. The turkey should be no more than 14 pounds. If the roasting pan is more than 2 inches larger than the turkey, the juices may burn. (If you use a larger pan, add a little broth to the pan as needed.) Always remove any bags or parts from the large and small cavities before cooking, and start with a clean oven to avoid excess smoking. Because I make my turkey broth months ahead of time and freeze it, I can use that for the bird and the gracious amount of gravy. After Thanksgiving, I make another broth or stock from the turkey bones, leftover skin, and parts. I even add any leftover gravy, and freeze the whole stock for yet again another turkey.**

1 onion, halved or quartered

2 to 3 garlic cloves

3 to 4 rosemary sprigs (optional)

1 (12- to 14-pound) turkey

¼ pound (1 stick) butter, melted, or vegetable oil (optional)

1 quart turkey broth or canned chicken broth

½ cup flour

1 cup cream (optional)

Salt

Freshly ground black pepper

Preheat the oven to 450°F.

Put the onion, garlic, and rosemary, if using, into the empty turkey cavity. Place the turkey in a large roasting pan, breast side up, and brush with butter or oil. Place in the oven, uncovered, and roast, unattended, for 1 hour. Carefully remove the turkey from the oven (close the door of the oven), watching out for the steam. Brush the turkey with butter or its juices. Return to the oven quickly and reduce the heat to 400°F. Roast another 30 minutes, checking the pan juices occasionally. Cover with foil if the breast is too brown. Cook another 30 minutes, adding stock if the pan juices evaporate.

The turkey is done when a meat thermometer inserted in its thigh registers 170°F. and the juices run clear. Let rest 10 minutes (the temperature should rise 10 degrees in 10 minutes). Remove the turkey to a board or platter for carving. Carve. Discard the onions and garlic from

inside the turkey. The turkey can be made a day ahead and refrigerated before reheating, carved, or it can be carved 10 minutes after resting.

If you decide to roast and carve the turkey ahead of time or if you want to freeze a portion of the turkey for another occasion, place the carved turkey in a shallow baking dish, cover it with broth, then wrap with foil or place the dish in a plastic bag; refrigerate for up to 2 days or freeze for up to 1 month. When you are ready to serve, defrost, if necessary; in the refrigerator, then bake in a 350°F. oven for 30 to 45 minutes or until heated completely through (or heat in the microwave).

While the turkey is resting, place the pan over medium-high heat. The skin, fat, and juices should be a beautiful dark bronze, not black. Remove all but ½ cup of the fat. Keep as much of the juices as possible. Whisk the flour into the fat and cook, stirring, until the flour turns light brown. Whisk in the rest of the

broth, and boil until thick and flavorful, stirring occasionally. Strain if lumpy or any part is burned. Add water or canned broth or stock if a thinner gravy is desired. Add as much cream as desired. Season to taste with salt and pepper.

*Tips: If the pan juices burn, make the gravy in a separate pan. Use ¼ pound (1 stick) butter instead of the fat in the pan. Cook the ½ cup flour in the butter and whisk in the broth and any of the pan juices that may still be good.*

*If you have one of those sturdy V-shaped roasting racks, you can try starting the turkey breast down, then turning it over halfway through its cooking time. This does seem to produce moister breast meat as well as a breast that's nicely browned, but it is almost impossible to turn a large turkey without one of those racks.*

# Yogurt Baked Chicken

Burt Wolf                                   Serves 4

One 2½- to 3-pound frying chicken, cut into 6 to 8 pieces

½ cup dry bread crumbs

¼ teaspoon salt

1 teaspoon garlic, finely minced

½ teaspoon paprika

¼ teaspoon curry powder

¼ teaspoon freshly ground black pepper

½ cup plain yogurt

Preheat the oven to 350°F. Line a shallow baking pan with heavy-duty aluminum foil and grease the foil lightly.

Rinse the chicken pieces and pat them dry. Remove the skin, if desired.

In a shallow plate, combine the bread crumbs, salt, garlic, paprika, curry powder and black pepper.

Place the yogurt in a shallow dish and lightly coat the chicken pieces in it. Dredge the pieces in the seasoned crumbs.

Arrange the chicken in the prepared pan and bake for 45 minutes, until cooked through.

Serve hot, or, if made ahead of time, serve cold. It's perfect for a picnic, eaten out of hand, like fried chicken.

# Chicken Bites with Sausages in a Vinegar Sauce
## Bocconcini di Pollo all'Aceto con Salsicce

Lidia Matticchio Bastianich                    Serves 6

**The sauce in this chicken dish should have a stick-to-the-finger quality when done. Chicken pieces on the bone can also be very good prepared this way—just keep in mind that they will need fifteen minutes additional cooking time and about a half cup more chicken stock than called for in this recipe. Serve the chicken with a nice big salad or a braised vegetable like escarole or broccoli.**

½ cup extra virgin olive oil

½ pound sweet Italian sausage, sliced (see Note)

2 pounds boneless, skinless chicken breasts, cut into 2-inch pieces

Salt

4 garlic cloves, finely chopped

2 teaspoons honey

2 tablespoons unsalted butter

¼ cup red wine vinegar

½ cup aromatic white wine, such as Gewürztraminer or Riesling

½ cup chicken stock or canned low-sodium chicken broth

2 tablespoons chopped fresh Italian parsley leaves

In a wide (at least 12-inch), heavy, nonreactive skillet, heat 2 tablespoons of the oil over medium heat. Add the sausage and cook, stirring often, until the sausage is lightly browned on all sides, about 3 minutes for thinner sausages and 5 minutes for fatter sausages.

Pour off the fat from the pan and add the remaining 2 tablespoons oil. Season the chicken pieces with salt and add them to the skillet. Cook the chicken, turning the pieces often, until light golden brown on all sides, about 4 minutes. About halfway through the cooking time, clear a small area on one side of the skillet and add the garlic to it. When the garlic is light golden brown, about 1 minute, stir it into the chicken-and-sausage mixture. Drizzle the honey over the chicken and sausage and cook, stirring constantly, until the chicken is a rich mahogany color, about 1 minute. Add the butter and stir until melted. Pour in the vinegar and bring it to a boil. Boil until the vinegar has almost entirely evaporated, about 2 minutes. Add the wine and bring to a boil, then add the chicken stock. Boil until the sauce is quite thick and there is just enough of it to barely coat the chicken pieces, about 2 minutes. Sprinkle the parsley over the chicken and serve.

*Note: For this I prefer luganica, a thin (½-inch-wide) pork sausage seasoned only with salt and pepper and without seeds of any kind. If unavailable, use the wider (1-inch-thick) sweet pork sausages, preferably without seeds. Cut the luganica into 1-inch lengths, the wider sausages into ½-inch slices.*

# Curried Chicken, Sweet Potatoes, and Bananas Wakaya

### Graham Kerr

**This delicious curry comes from the Indo-Fijian population of the islands, while the sauce captures the intriguing, mysterious flavor of the tamarind. To me, the sweet and sour taste sensations contained within the tamarind fruit captures the zest of the island of Wakaya. If you have trouble finding tamarind pods to make the sauce, you can substitute a good mango chutney and add a little fresh lemon juice. I know the preparation for this dish appears to be complicated, but the actual labor is quite light. An unusual, attractive curry…and easy to make!**

## Tamarind Sauce

- 1½ ounces or about 15 inches peeled tamarind pods
- 1 teaspoon light olive oil
- ¼ teaspoon yellow mustard seeds
- 1 teaspoon cumin seeds
- ¼ teaspoon garam masala
- ⅛ teaspoon cayenne pepper (optional)
- 5 quarter-size slices fresh gingerroot
- 3 ounces pitted dates (about 12)
- 1 mango, peeled and cubed

## Chicken

- ¾ teaspoon India Ethmix (recipe follows) or good Madras curry powder
- 3 boneless chicken breasts, skin on, about 6 ounces each
- 2 teaspoons light olive oil

## Curry

- 2 heads bok choy
- 3 bananas
- ⅓ cup fresh lemon juice
- 12 ounces steamed sweet potato, peeled, halved, and cut into 1-inch pieces
- 1 teaspoon arrowroot
- ½ cup low-sodium chicken or vegetable stock

### To prepare the tamarind sauce

Cut the peeled tamarind pods into small pieces and soak in ½ cup warm water for 15 minutes. Strain, reserving the liquid and pulp, and discard the seeds.

Warm the oil in a small frying pan over medium-high heat. Add the mustard and cumin seeds and cook for 2 minutes. Transfer to a blender or food processor.

Add the garam masala, optional cayenne pepper, ginger, and the reserved tamarind pulp and liquid. Process at high speed for 1 minute. Add the dates and mango and continue blending for another minute. Press the sauce through a strainer with a purée press or large spoon. Set aside until ready to use.

### To prepare the chicken

Rub ½ teaspoon of the India Ethmix or curry powder into the skinless side of each of the chicken breasts.

Warm the oil in a large frying pan over medium-high heat. Sauté the breasts, skin side down, for 2 minutes. Turn the breasts and cook for another 3 minutes. Turn twice more, cooking for a total of 9 minutes, or until just cooked through.

Remove from the pan and set aside. Do not wash the pan.

### To prepare the curry

Cut the leaves off the bok choy stems and wash well. Steam the leaves for 1 minute and cool immediately under cold running water. Drain well and pat dry; set aside to use as a bed for the curry.

Cut off and discard the tough bottoms of the bok choy stems. Slice the tender parts of the stems into ½-inch strips. Set aside for the garnish.

Peel the bananas and cut into 1-inch pieces. Coat the pieces with the lemon juice in a large bowl to keep them from turning brown. Gently toss the sweet potato pieces with the bananas and transfer to a large steamer. Cover and steam for 5 minutes to heat through. Combine the arrowroot with the stock to make a slurry.

Reheat the oil and chicken cooking juices remaining in the large frying pan. Add the garlic and India Ethmix and stir just long enough to heat through. Deglaze the pan with the arrowroot slurry, loosening the flavorful bits from the bottom.

2 cloves garlic, peeled, bashed, and chopped

2 teaspoons India Ethmix or good Madras curry powder

½ cup yogurt cheese (see page 135)

4 green onions, white and green parts, cut into ¼-inch slices

**Garnish**

1 mango, peeled and sliced

½ English cucumber, unpeeled cut into very thin strips

12 small radishes

Spoon the yogurt cheese into a 2-cup glass measure. Add a little of the hot stock and mix well to temper the yogurt. Whisk in the rest of the stock to make a smooth, creamy sauce.

Combine the curry sauce with the hot bananas and sweet potatoes in a high-sided skillet. Keep warm but do not boil.

Remove and discard the skin from the chicken and cut the meat into 1-inch pieces. Gently stir the chicken and onions into the banana mixture over medium-high heat.

**To serve**

Arrange two or three bok choy leaves on each dinner plate. Place a serving of the curry on the bok choy leaves and garnish with the bok choy strips, mango slices, cucumber strips, and radishes. Spoon a dollop of tamarind sauce or mango chutney on the side as a condiment.

## India Ethmix

Makes about ½ cup

**This handy blend can be made in just a few minutes and stored in a sealed jar for use in a variety of dishes.**

5 teaspoons turmeric

1½ teaspoons dry mustard

5 teaspoons ground cumin

5 teaspoons ground coriander

1¼ teaspoons cayenne pepper

2½ teaspoons dill seeds

2½ teaspoons decorticated cardamom seeds

2½ teaspoons fenugreek seeds

Grind to a fine powder in a small electric coffee grinder designated for this use. Shake through a sieve to remove coarse pieces or debris.

# Desserts and Breads

## WITH NATHALIE DUPREE

Nathalie Dupree trained at London's Cordon Bleu and has cooked at restaurants in Europe, but her heart has always belonged to the South. A long-time resident of Georgia, she ran her own restaurant and founded Rich's Cooking School in Atlanta before launching one of the most enduring cooking show careers in public television. From her first series, *New Southern Cooking*, in 1986, to her latest, *Nathalie Dupree Entertains,* as well as in her eight cookbooks, she has taught us that cooking should be fun and relaxed, and that enjoying good food and your guests is more important than achieving perfection. "If you've watched my television show, you know that perfect is not my thing!" she writes in *Comfortable Entertaining*, the James Beard Award–winning companion cookbook to her current series.

Although Nathalie can turn out a flaky Angel Biscuit as well as any Southerner, her culinary repertoire is inspired from cuisines around the world, from Italy to Morocco to Mexico, and her menus and entertainment tips are for anyone on either side of the Mason-Dixon Line. Certainly the Southern way with—and appreciation for—desserts, sweet treats, and breads deserves to become a national trend.

# Chocolate-Nut Pie

Nathalie Dupree                                                    Serves 8

## Pie Crust

1¼ cups all-purpose flour

½ teaspoon salt

¼ cup vegetable shortening

¼ cup butter

3 to 8 tablespoons ice water

## Filling

4 ounces semi-sweet or bittersweet chocolate

3 large eggs, lightly beaten

1 cup light corn syrup

1 cup sugar

2 tablespoons butter, melted and cooled

1 teaspoon vanilla extract

2 cups macadamia nuts or pecans

## Garnish

Grated white chocolate or powdered sugar

Lightly sweetened whipped cream

### For the pie crust

Combine the flour and salt in the bowl of a food processor and pulse several times to mix. Cut the shortening and butter into small pieces and add to the dough. Pulse until the size of cornmeal. Add 3 to 4 tablespoons of ice water and continue to pulse the dough until it starts to clump together (adding additional water in small amounts if necessary). Do not let it form a ball or it will be tough.

Remove the dough, form into a ball, and press into a flattened disk. Wrap and chill for 30 minutes or up to 3 days.

Flour a board and roll out the dough until you have a disk ⅛ inch thick and 1½ inches larger than your pan. Fold in quarters.

Place the pastry in a 9-inch pie pan with the tip of the triangle in the center and unfold. Trim the pastry 1 inch larger than the pie pan and fold the overhanging pastry under itself. Press the tines of a fork around the edge. To make a fluted pattern, use both of your thumbs to pinch the dough all around the rim so that the edge of the dough stands up. Wrap and place in the freezer or refrigerator for 30 minutes or up to 3 days.

### For the filling

Preheat the oven to 350°F. Coarsely chop the chocolate, then melt it slowly in a heavy pot over low heat or in the microwave. Spread it evenly over the bottom of the chilled pie shell

In a large bowl, mix the eggs, corn syrup, sugar, butter, and vanilla until fully incorporated. Stir in the nuts, then pour the mixture into the chocolate-lined pie shell. Bake on the middle rack of the oven for 45 to 50 minutes or until the filling is set. Remove the pie to a rack and allow to cool.

### For the garnish

Once the pie has cooled, cut a leaf stencil or other design from a piece of cardboard and place it over the pie. Sprinkle the pie with grated white chocolate or powdered sugar. Cut wedges of the pie and serve with lightly sweetened whipped cream.

*Note: The pie can be made ahead and frozen or stored at room temperature for several days.*

# Double Chocolate Pudding

Todd English                                              Serves 6

1½ cups heavy cream

1 cup milk

½ cup sugar

Pinch salt

3 tablespoons Dutch processed cocoa powder

2 teaspoons cornstarch

1 large egg

2 large egg yolks

5 ounces semi-sweet chocolate, finely chopped

2 tablespoons unsalted butter, cut into small pieces and softened at room temperature

2 tablespoons instant espresso powder or double strong coffee

1 tablespoon hot water

1 teaspoon vanilla extract

Place 1 cup cream, 1 cup milk and ¼ cup sugar and salt in a saucepan and bring to a boil over medium heat.

Place the cocoa, cornstarch and remaining ¼ cup sugar in a mixing bowl and stir to combine. Add the remaining ½ cup cream and mix until smooth and free of lumps.

Place the hot cream mixture into the cocoa mixture and bring to a boil over medium heat for 2 minutes, stirring.

Place the eggs and egg yolks in a bowl and slowly whisk. Add 1 cup of the hot cream and cocoa mixture to the eggs and whisk well. Add the egg-hot cream and cocoa mixture back into the hot cream and cocoa mixture, whisking all the while. Cook over medium low heat, whisking well, until it becomes thick, about 3–5 minutes. Do not allow it to boil.

Transfer to the bowl of a mixer fitted with a paddle attachment. Add the chocolate and butter all at once and beat on low until completely cooled. Cover and refrigerate. Serve garnished with whipped cream.

# Chocolate Raspberry Cheesecake

Debbi Fields                                                    Serves 12

The flavors of chocolate and raspberry were meant for each other, so it seemed only natural to combine them in one luscious dessert. This cake is as pretty to look at as it is good to eat, and it is intense with raspberry flavor. The raspberry flavor here comes from raspberry liqueur, also known as *framboise*, and is further heightened by a garnish of raspberry puree and fresh berries.

I always want you to take care melting chocolate. No matter which method you choose, the chocolate should be absolutely smooth when you're done.

## Crust

- 1 cup chocolate wafer crumbs
- 2 tablespoons sugar
- 2 tablespoons all-purpose flour
- 4 tablespoons (½ stick) unsalted butter, melted

## Filling

- 24 ounces cream cheese, softened
- ½ cup sugar
- 4 large eggs, at room temperature
- 8 ounces semisweet chocolate, melted.
- ¼ cup raspberry liqueur
- ½ cup heavy cream
- 1 tablespoon pure vanilla extract

## Topping

- 1 cup sour cream
- ⅓ cup firmly packed light brown sugar

## Sauce

- 12 ounces frozen sweetened raspberries, thawed
- ¼ cup sugar
- 1 tablespoon raspberry liqueur
- 2 pints fresh raspberries (optional)

Preheat the oven to 300 degrees F. Lightly butter the springform pan.

**Make the crust**

In a bowl, combine the chocolate wafer crumbs, sugar, and flour, and stir in the butter until combined. Press the crust over the bottom and up the sides of the prepared pan. Bake for 15 minutes. Set the pan aside to cool.

**Make the filling**

Put the cream cheese and sugar in a large bowl and beat until smooth using the electric mixer on medium speed. Scrape down the bowl. Add the eggs, 1 at a time, beating for 20 seconds after each addition. Scrape down the bowl. Add the melted chocolate, raspberry liqueur, cream, and vanilla, and beat until smooth. Scrape down the bowl. Pour the filling into the prepared crust and smooth the top.

Fill a 2-quart baking pan halfway with hot water and place on the bottom rack of the oven. Bake the cake on the middle rack for 1 hour. Lower the oven temperature to 275

degrees F. and bake 1 hour more. Turn off the oven and leave the cake in for 30 minutes with the door closed. Remove the cake to a wire rack and cool to room temperature.

**Make the topping**

In a bowl, combine the sour cream and sugar until smooth. Pour over the top of the cake and spread until smooth. Cover the cake with foil and chill for at least 4 hours or overnight.

**Make the sauce**

Combine all the sauce ingredients and puree until smooth in the food processor. Strain the puree through a fine-mesh sieve into a bowl, cover, and chill until cold.

To serve, top the cake with fresh raspberries, if desired, and pour half of the sauce over them. Serve the remaining sauce separately. Or ladle a pool of the sauce onto each dessert plate and arrange a slice of the cheesecake on it.

*Equipment Needed: 9-inch springform pan, electric mixer, food processor with metal blade*

# Super Moist Carrot Cake

John D. Folse                                                    Serves 8 to 10

3 cups grated carrots

2 cups sugar

1½ cups vegetable oil

4 eggs

2 cups all purpose flour

3 teaspoons baking powder

3 teaspoons baking soda

1 teaspoon salt

2 teaspoons cinnamon

1 tablespoon vanilla

1 cup chopped pecans

1 (20-ounce) can crushed pineapple

1 cup sugar

2½ tablespoons cornstarch

8 ounces cream cheese

½ stick butter

1 pound powdered sugar

Preheat oven to 350 degrees F. Oil and flour four 9-inch cake pans. Set aside. In a large mixing bowl, cream sugar and oil until well blended. Add eggs, one at a time, whipping after each addition. In a separate bowl, combine flour, baking powder, soda, salt and cinnamon. Add, a little at a time, into the egg mixture, blending well until all is incorporated. Fold in ½ tablespoon of the vanilla, pecans and grated carrots. Once all is well blended, pour evenly into the four cake pans. Bake 30–40 minutes or until cake tester comes out clean. While cake is baking, make filling by combining pineapple, sugar and cornstarch. Bring to a low boil over medium-high heat, stirring constantly for 5 minutes. Once mixture thickens, remove filling from heat and allow it to cool. In the bowl of an electric mixer, combine cream cheese, butter, powdered sugar and the remaining vanilla. Blend on a low speed until well mixed. Increase speed and whip until icing is fluffy and smooth. Remove and set aside. When cakes are done, remove from oven and allow to cool. Remove from baking pans and spread pineapple filling between layers. Ice with the cream cheese frosting and serve.

# Mango Ice Cream Sandwich with Macadamia Nut Cookies and Tropical Fruit Compote

Roy Yamaguchi                    Serves 6

**A glorified ice cream sandwich, this recipe takes advantage of the abundance of mangoes in Hawaii, although it works equally well when made with strawberries, blueberries or guava.**

## Cookie Dough

- 1 pound unsalted butter
- 1⅔ cups granulated sugar
- 2 eggs
- ¼ teaspoon vanilla extract
- 3⅓ cups all-purpose flour
- ⅛ teaspoon salt
- ½ cup Hawaiian macadamia nuts, chopped

## Mango Ice Cream

- ¾ cup half-and-half
- ⅔ cup granulated sugar
- 3 yolks
- 1 cup heavy cream
- ¾ cup puree of mango, or strawberries, blueberries or guava

## Tropical Fruit Compote

- 1 ripe mango
- 4 kiwi fruit
- ¼ fresh pineapple, or 1 cup chunked pineapple
- Sugar or honey to taste

## Garnish

- Sprigs of mint
- Tropical flowers

**Preparation of the cookie dough**

Preheat the oven to 350°F. In a medium bowl, cream the butter and sugar for 3 to 4 minutes, until the mixture is light and fluffy.

Beat in the eggs and vanilla. Fold in the flour, salt and nuts, and mix for 2 minutes, until a smooth dough forms.

Roll the cookie dough ⅛ inch thick, cut into rounds and bake them on an ungreased, lined sheet pan for 10 to 15 minutes, or until they are lightly browned around the edges.

**Preparation of the mango ice cream**

Bring the half-and-half and sugar to a boil in a medium saucepan. Slowly pour the hot mixture into the egg yolks in a stainless-steel double boiler. Cook the mixture slowly, stirring continuously for 2 to 3 minutes in order to form a custard.

Cool the custard. Stir in the heavy cream and the mango puree, and freeze the mixture according to the directions for your ice cream machine.

**Preparation of the tropical fruit compote**

Cut the fruits in consistent sizes. Mix them together in a medium bowl, and sweeten to taste with the sugar or honey.

**Assembly**

Sandwich a ½-cup scoop of the ice cream between two cookies, and flatten the ice cream slightly.

Ladle a pool of the mango puree on the center of each plate. Cut the ice cream cookie sandwiches in half and place them split-open on the plate.

Spoon the tropical fruit compote over the apex of the sandwich, so that it spills onto the plate and the pool of mango puree.

Garnish each dish with a fresh sprig of mint and a tropical flower.

*Wine Suggestion: Williams & Selyem "Allen" Pinot Noir, Russian River Valley, California, or Gigondas, "Domaine du Cayron," Michel Faraud, Rhone Valley, France*

# Debbi's Flourless Fudge Brownies

Debbi Fields                                        Serves 12

You'll need a total of 22 ounces of chocolate for these brownies, which gives you some idea of how wonderfully rich they are! And, yes, they are flourless, so they won't rise the way other brownies do in the pan. These are dense and delicious—there's nothing cakelike about them—and as the recipe indicates, they must be made in advance, chilled, and then brought back almost to room temperature for you to experience their incredible flavor and texture. High-quality chocolate makes them even better.

6 large eggs

18 ounces semisweet chocolate, chopped

16 tablespoons (2 sticks) unsalted butter, cut into tablespoons

1 teaspoon pure vanilla extract

**Glaze**

¼ cup heavy cream

4 ounces semisweet chocolate, chopped

24 pecan halves, toasted, for topping

Preheat the oven to 425 degrees F. Butter the baking pan, line it with aluminum foil, and butter the foil. Set the eggs in a bowl and cover them with hot tap water.

In the top of a double boiler set over barely simmering water, melt the chocolate with the butter, stirring until smooth. Stir in the vanilla. Transfer the mixture to a bowl and let it cool slightly on a rack.

Put the warm eggs in a large bowl and beat using the electric mixer on high speed until about triple in volume, about 5 minutes. Fold half of the beaten eggs into the chocolate mixture to lighten it. Gently fold in the remaining beaten eggs. Scrape the batter into the prepared pan and smooth the top.

Set the pan of batter in a larger baking pan. Pour hot water into the larger pan to come halfway up the sides of the brownie pan.

Bake the brownies on the middle rack of the oven for 10 minutes. Turn off the oven and let the

brownies stand in the oven for 5 minutes. Remove the brownies from the water-bath to a wire rack and let stand while you make the glaze.

**Make the glaze**

In a small ceramic or glass bowl covered with plastic wrap, heat the cream with the chocolate on High in a microwave oven for 30-second intervals, stirring after each interval, until smooth.

Pour the hot glaze evenly over the surface of the brownies. Spread it with a rubber spatula until smooth and let cool completely. When cool, cover the pan with plastic wrap and refrigerate until well chilled and firm, about 4 hours, or overnight.

To serve, cut into 12 squares and top each with pecans. Arrange the brownies on a serving plate. For the best flavor and texture, let the brownies stand at room temperature 20 to 30 minutes before serving.

*Equipment Needed: 9-inch square baking pan, electric mixer*

# Bread Pudding and Whiskey Sauce

Brennan's Executive Chef Michael Roussel

Serves 15 to 18

½ cup raisins

4 cups milk

1 cup heavy cream

4 large eggs

1½ cups sugar

½ cup chopped pecans

1 teaspoon cinnamon

1 teaspoon nutmeg

1 teaspoon vanilla

1 stale loaf French bread, about 14 ounces

6 tablespoons butter plus extra for buttering baking dish.

Whiskey sauce (recipe follows)

Place the raisins in a small bowl and add warm water to cover. Soak for 2 hours, then drain.

Preheat oven to 350 degrees F.

In a large mixing bowl, combine the milk, cream, eggs, sugar, raisins, and pecans. Whisk the mixture until well blended, then stir in the cinnamon, nutmeg, and vanilla. Break the bread into the bowl and fold the mixture until the bread is soggy.

Butter a large loaf pan or 13x9x2-inch baking dish and pour in the bread mixture. Push 6 tablespoons of butter into the top of the loaf and set the pan in a larger pan filled with about ½-inch of water. Bake the bread pudding in the water bath for 30 minutes, then remove the larger pan from the oven; bake the bread pudding for another 45 minutes.

Slice the bread pudding and serve warm topped with whiskey sauce.

## Whiskey Sauce

Makes 1 cup

3 large eggs

1 cup sugar

1 teaspoon vanilla

½ cup milk

1 tablespoon cornstarch

¼ cup cold water

3 tablespoons Canadian whiskey

Place the eggs in a large saucepan and whisk over medium heat until slightly thickened. Add the sugar, vanilla, and milk and cook until hot; do not let the mixture come to a boil.

In a small bowl, blend the cornstarch into ¼ cup cold water. Stir the cornstarch into the egg mixture, stirring constantly. Add the whiskey and cook the sauce over medium heat until smooth and thick enough to coat the back of a spoon, about 15 minutes; stir frequently.

Serve the whiskey sauce either at room temperature, or chill and serve cold.

# Creamy Summer Berry and Lemon Gratin

Joanne Weir                                                           Serves 6 to 8

**Every time I teach this dessert in class, I have students almost licking their plates. It's creamy, not too sweet, lemony, and comforting—everything a dessert should be. It can also be made with peaches or nectarines, and in the winter, you can make it with blood or navel orange sections.**

4 lemons

1½ cups whole milk

5 egg yolks

1 teaspoon cornstarch

⅓ cup sugar

2 tablespoons all-purpose flour

½ teaspoon vanilla extract

1 tablespoon lemon juice

1 tablespoon unsalted butter, at room temperature

½ cup mascarpone

4 cups mixed berries, blueberries, blackberries, raspberries, boysenberries

2 tablespoons confectioners' sugar

Peel the lemons with a vegetable peeler avoiding the white pith. Scald the milk in a saucepan over medium heat. Add the lemon peel and remove from the heat. Let sit for 1 hour. After 1 hour, strain the milk to remove the lemon peel and discard the peel.

In a bowl, beat the egg yolks until light and fluffy. In another bowl, combine the cornstarch, sugar, and flour. Add this mixture to the egg yolks and beat until light and fluffy, about 1 minute.

Scald the milk a second time and add the warm milk slowly to the eggs, whisking constantly. Place the mixture back in the saucepan and over low heat, stirring, cook until the mixture thickens and bubbles around the edges. Remove from the heat and whisk in the vanilla, lemon juice, and butter. Fold in the mascarpone until well mixed.

Preheat the broiler.

Divide the custard mixture among 6 or 8 individual gratin or tartlet dishes, 5 inches in diameter. Press the berries into the custard mixture. Sift the confectioners' sugar over the top. Broil until the tops are golden brown, 1 to 2 minutes. Serve hot or at room temperature.

# Blintzes with Strawberries

### Graham Kerr

**I can never think of New York without thinking of blintzes—those creamy, comforting packets oozing with cheese and butter and fat. Rather than deprive myself of this quintessential New York treat, I have managed to retain the creamy texture and luxurious taste while tossing out a good number of calories. The sauce is a pleasantly piquant strawberry salsa with a surprising edge that people seem to love.**

## Crêpe Batter

- 1 whole egg
- 1 egg yolk
- 1 cup skim milk
- ½ cup all-purpose flour
- 1 teaspoon light olive oil

## Strawberry Salsa

- 3 cups chopped fresh strawberries (about 2 pints whole berries)
- 1 medium crisp apple, unpeeled, chopped (about 1 cup)
- 1 small jalapeño pepper, cored, seeded, and finely chopped
- 1 tablespoon sugar
- ⅛ teaspoon freshly ground black pepper

## Crêpe Filling

- ¾ cup yogurt cheese (recipe follows)
- ¼ cup chopped dried strawberries
- 2 teaspoons maple syrup
- ¼ teaspoon vanilla extract
- 2 teaspoons cornstarch

To prepare the crêpe batter, beat the whole egg, egg yolk, and milk in a large bowl. Whisk in the flour and oil. Let the batter rest for 30 minutes before cooking.

While the batter is resting, prepare the salsa. In a small bowl, combine the chopped strawberries, apple, and jalapeño. Sprinkle with the sugar and black pepper and set aside.

To prepare the filling, gently combine the yogurt cheese, dried strawberries, maple syrup, vanilla, and cornstarch in a small bowl. Set aside while you cook the crêpes.

To cook the crêpes, spray a medium crêpe pan or skillet with cooking spray and warm over medium heat. It is important that the skillet be good and warm before adding the batter. Pour a scant ¼ cup of the batter into the pan, gently tilting the pan back and forth to coat the bottom with batter. When the top dulls and bubbles form, 30 to 45 seconds, flip the crêpe onto a paper towel, cooked side up. The crêpe will be a pale golden color on the cooked side.

Repeat this process with the remaining batter, spraying the skillet with cooking spray if needed to keep the crêpes from sticking. You may go ahead and fill each crêpe while the next one is cooking, or you may stack the finished crêpes until ready to fill.

To fill the blintzes, spoon 2 generous tablespoons of the filling into the center of the cooked side of a crêpe. Fold the edges in toward the center to make a small square envelope. Repeat with the remaining crêpes. If they will not be cooked immediately, store the blintzes seam side down in a single layer in a shallow container. They will keep in the refrigerator overnight.

When ready to cook the blintzes, preheat the broiler. Spray a baking sheet with cooking spray and lay the filled crêpes on the baking sheet, seam side down. Spray the tops of the blintzes with cooking spray and broil for 5 minute, or until golden brown.

To serve, spread a generous ½ cup of the salsa on each dessert plate. Lay a hot blintz on top of the salsa.

*Making Crêpes: The key to making good crêpes is the temperature of the pan. You'll need to experiment with your stove and your cookware, but try to reach a true medium temperature that will keep the pan at a consistent temperature.*

## Yogurt Cheese

1½ cups plain nonfat yogurt, no gelatin added

Put the yogurt in a strainer over a bowl. Or you can use a coffee filter, piece of muslin, or a paper towel and place it in a small sieve over a bowl. Cover and let drain in the refrigerator for 12 hours or overnight. It becomes quite firm and the small lumps disappear, which makes it ideal for use in sauce. The liquid whey drains into the bowl, leaving you with thick, creamy yogurt cheese.

# Roast Caramelized Pears

Jacques Pépin                                                    Serves 4

**The success of desserts with pears depends largely on their quality and ripeness. For this recipe, Anjou or Bartlett pears are roasted at a high temperature for more than 1 hour, until their juices caramelize and turn a rich mahogany color. The juices are then diluted with a little Madeira wine, and the pears are served at room temperature with the Madeira juices.**

4 Anjou or Bartlett pears with stems (about 2 pounds), all of equal ripeness

2 teaspoons unsalted butter

1 tablespoon lemon juice

¼ cup sugar

3 tablespoons Madeira wine

Mint leaves, for decoration

Preheat the oven to 425 degrees.

Do not remove the stems from the pears, but peel them with a vegetable peeler. Then, using a melon baller, citrus spoon, or half-teaspoon measuring spoon, remove the seeds from each pear by digging them out from the base.

Melt the butter in a small gratin dish. Stir the lemon juice into the butter. Roll the pears in this mixture and sprinkle them with the sugar.

Stand the pears upright in the gratin dish, and place them in the preheated 425-degree oven. Cook the pears for about 1¼ hours, basting them with their own cooking juices every 15 or 20 minutes, until they are nicely browned and tender when pierced with the point of a knife. The juices should be caramelized and a rich brown color at the end of the cooking; if they should begin to burn, prevent this by immediately adding 3 to 4 tablespoons of water to the gratin dish.

When the pears are tender, remove them from the oven. Add the Madeira to the dish, and stir well to combine it with the juices.

Cool the pears to room temperature. Serve them with the accumulated juices spooned over and around them. Decorate with mint leaves.

# Caramel-Dipped Fruit

Jacques Torres                              Makes 1 pound dipped fruit

**This is a very easy treat to make. You can use any kind of fruit. I like to make my fruit skewers with fruit combinations that are colorful and tasty. Be creative! If you use refrigerated fruit, allow it to come to room temperature a few hours before dipping it in the hot caramel. If you use cold fruit, condensation will form, creating moisture that will cause the sugar to melt. It is best to make these within three hours of the time you plan to serve them. Since fruit is mostly water, its moisture will cause the sugar to melt, which makes the treats sticky and gooey. When working with caramel, be sure to have a bowl of cold water on hand. If you get hot sugar on your fingers, immediately dip them in cold water to remove it and avoid a burn.**

Scant ½ cup water

Generous 2¼ cups granulated sugar

Scant ⅔ cup light corn syrup

16 ounces fresh fruit

*Tip: To cool a hot thermometer, stand it upright in a tall container. Do not put in cold water, or it will break. Keeping it upright ensures the mercury will not separate as it cools. I usually buy the thermometers that come in a metal casing or cage. Always hang your thermometer when it is time to store it.*

Place the water, sugar, and corn syrup in a 2-quart heavy-bottomed saucepan over medium-high heat. The corn syrup will make the cooked sugar harder and crunchier; it will also help prevent the cooked sugar from melting as quickly when it reacts to the humidity in the air. Insert a candy thermometer and cook the sugar mixture to 311°F, what is known as the hard crack stage. Stir the sugar slowly as it cooks to ensure that it cooks evenly. If you do not stir it, the mixture will develop hot spots and the sugar will cook faster in those spots. Use a pastry brush to keep the inside of the saucepan clean as the sugar cooks, or the sugar may recrystallize. To do this, dip a clean brush in cold water and brush the inside of the pan clean.

Remove the cooked sugar from the heat and pour it into a medium-size heatproof glass bowl. The glass bowl will hold the temperature and stop the cooking process. It will also allow you to reheat the sugar in the microwave if necessary. If you leave the sugar in the saucepan, the sugar will continue to cook and turn dark

brown. Occasionally stir the hot sugar to keep it from darkening due to the residual heat. Stirring also helps to keep its temperature even. I put a towel under the bowl to keep it from tipping and to protect my hands from the heat of the glass.

Peel, core or pit, and halve the fruit as necessary. Use a sharp knife to slice the fruit into small pieces. (This is not necessary for berries or grapes.) Arrange the fruit on toothpicks or small skewers in any combination you like. Leave enough room at one end of the toothpick or skewer so you will be able to hold it as you dip it in the hot sugar. Dip each toothpick in the hot sugar, coating the fruits completely. Wipe the toothpick against the rim of the bowl to remove any excess sugar and place on a sheet of parchment paper. Repeat until all of the fruit has been dipped. The fruit skewers should release easily from the parchment paper as soon as they cool. You can arrange them on a plate or use your imagination to make a fruit skewer centerpiece.

# Lemon Blueberry Pie

Madeleine Kamman                                            Serves 8

**The producer-director of the TV series _Madeleine Cooks_ thinks this is the best lemon tart in the world.**

### For the Pastry

- 1 cup sifted flour
- 1 tablespoon sugar
- 6 tablespoons butter
- 1 teaspoon grated lime rind
- 2½ tablespoons water

### For the Filling

- 5 tablespoons butter
- ½ cup sugar
- 1 teaspoon cornstarch
- Juice of 3 lemons and 2 limes
- Pinch of salt
- ½ teaspoon each grated lime rind and lemon rind
- 2 eggs
- 2 egg yolks
- 1 tablespoon Jack Daniel's

### For the Topping

- 1 pint blueberries
- 1 egg white
- ¼ cup sugar
- 1 teaspoon cornstarch
- ½ teaspoon grated lime rind
- 2 tablespoons lime juice
- 1½ tablespoons Jack Daniel's

Put the flour, the sugar, and the butter cut into tablespoon pieces in a food processor container. Add the lime rind and 2 tablespoons of water. Process for 55 seconds to obtain a ball of dough. Add the remainder of the water only if needed. Flatten into a ½-inch-thick, 4-inch-wide piece of dough. Refrigerate for 30 minutes.

To prepare the filling, cream the butter, add the sugar, cornstarch, citrus juices, salt, rinds, eggs, egg yolks, and Jack Daniel's. Mix well. If the mixture looks separated, it does not matter.

Roll out the pastry into an 8-inch pie plate. Prebake the shell for 10 minutes in a preheated 400° oven. Fill with the lemon cream and finish baking until golden, about 15 minutes. Cool in the pie plate.

Reserve 24 large blueberries. Dip 12 of them in the egg white and roll in 1 tablespoon of the sugar. Let dry on a plate. Alternate the 12 sugar-dipped berries with 12 undipped berries around the edges of the pie.

Mix the remaining blueberries with the remaining sugar, the cornstarch, lime rind and lime juice. Cook until a sauce forms and thickens. Serve each pie wedge with one large spoonful of the blueberry sauce.

# Kris's Apple Crisp

Jacques Torres        Makes one 8-inch casserole; about 8 servings

**This is a good dessert for any beginner to make. On our team, we decide the difficulty of a dessert based on whether we think Kris can do it. If she can, the rating is *Easy*. She doesn't cook or bake very often, but when she does, this is what she makes. I create fancy desserts all day at work, but when it is my turn to choose, this one is always on my list. Kris likes to use McIntosh apples for this recipe, but you can use any kind you like. If you like ice cream even a little bit, serve it with this dessert—apple crisp without ice cream is like cookies without milk!**

10 McIntosh apples

¾ cup unbleached all-purpose flour

½ cup granulated sugar

½ cup firmly packed light
 brown sugar

½ cup cold unsalted butter, cubed

 Pinch of ground cinnamon

 Pinch of salt

 Pinch of freshly grated nutmeg

½ cup pecans or walnuts, chopped

¼ cup apple cider (optional)

 Vanilla ice cream

Preheat the oven to 350°F. Use a sharp paring knife or apple peeler to peel the apples. Slice them in half and remove the cores, then slice the apple halves into thick segments. Kris likes to use thinner slices and I prefer chunks. Set aside.

Combine the flour, sugars, butter, cinnamon, salt, and nutmeg in a large mixing bowl. Use a pastry blender to cut the butter into the blended ingredients. The finished mixture should be crumbly, and you will be able to see small chunks of butter in it. Mix in the chopped nuts. Do this after you work in the butter so you won't have to crunch through the nuts.

Lightly spray an 8-inch casserole or soufflé dish with vegetable cooking spray. Fill the dish about half full with the apples. Add about half of the apple cider and cover with a generous portion of the flour mixture. Top with the remaining apples and

cider. The apples should mound over the top of the dish because they will shrink as they bake. Cover with the remaining flour mixture. Place in the oven and bake, covered, for about 30 minutes. Then uncover and bake until the topping is a dark golden brown and appears dry, about an additional 30 minutes. Remove from the oven and spoon into small bowls. I always serve it warm with vanilla ice cream so the ice cream melts into the apple crisp.

We usually make a double batch. You can freeze the baked apple crisp well wrapped in plastic wrap. When ready, allow it to thaw. If I am going to reheat the whole dish, I do it in the oven at 350°F for 20 to 30 minutes. Otherwise, spoon it into small bowls and reheat each bowl in the microwave on high power for 60 to 90 seconds.

# Burnt-Cream Custard with Grand Marnier
## Crème Brûlée au Grand Marnier

Pierre Franey                                                    Serves 6

---

**I don't think anything as good as a *crème brûlée* will ever go out of style. Here's the one we cooked at La Reserve in Albi. It's a good idea to buy the type of brown sugar that pours easily and then force it through a strainer to make doubly sure you eliminate any lumps.**

---

6 egg yolks

½ cup sugar

2⅓ cups cream

½ cup milk

⅓ cup Crème de Grand Marnier

¼ cup brown sugar

Preheat oven to 350°.

In a large mixing bowl, whisk together the egg yolks and sugar and beat until the mixture turns a light lemony color. Add the cream, the milk, and the Crème de Grand Marnier and combine well.

Arrange 6 individual-serving-size ramekins (preferably ¾ inch deep by 4½ inches in diameter) side by side in a large roasting pan. Fill each with ⅔ cup of the mixture. Pour hot water to the depth of ¼ inch into the roasting pan around them.

Bake for 20 to 25 minutes, or until the mixture has set but is still creamy. Do not overcook.

Allow the ramekins to cool at room temperature until they are no longer steaming. Chill the ramekins.

About 1 hour before serving, remove ramekins from refrigerator to take off the chill. Just before serving, preheat the broiler to the highest setting.

Sprinkle each ramekin evenly with 2 teaspoons brown sugar. Place them under the broiler until the sugar is caramelized and has turned dark brown. Rotate them as necessary to brown the sugar evenly.

# Coconut Pancakes
## *Abele*

Madhur Jaffrey                                                  Serves 6

**This dessert combines the crêpe of the Western world with a delicious cardamom-flavored coconut-cashew filling which could only come out of the tropical East. Only fresh coconut should be used for the filling.**

**For the Batter**

1 scant cup all-purpose flour

A pinch of salt

1 large egg plus 1 egg yolk

1¼ cups milk

1 tablespoon melted butter

¼ teaspoon ground cardamom

**For the Filling**

1½ cups freshly grated coconut

⅓ cup chopped, roasted, unsalted cashews

8 tablespoons dark brown sugar

¼ teaspoon ground cardamom

2 tablespoons golden raisins

**You Also Need**

3 to 4 tablespoons vegetable oil

1 juicy lemon

Put all the ingredients for the batter in the container of an electric blender. Blend until smooth. Set aside for at least 30 minutes. Empty into a bowl. Have ready a ladle that will pick up about 4–5 tablespoons of the batter.

Combine all the ingredients for the filling. Set aside.

Brush a 7-inch crêpe pan or a non-stick frying pan with a little oil and set over medium heat. When smoking hot, pour in 4–5 tablespoons of the batter. Quickly tilt the pan in all directions so that the batter flows to the ends and forms a thin film. (Any extra batter may be poured back into the bowl.)

Cook the pancake for a few minutes until the bottom has some brown spots and the edges can be lifted. Turn the pancake over with a spatula and cook for another minute. Remove and put on a plate. Start to make the second pancake as you made the first. As it cooks, put 2–3 tablespoons of filling on the first pancake, squeeze a generous amount of lemon juice over that and roll it up. Keep it in a covered dish. Make all the pancakes this way, keeping them in a single layer. When they are all made, you could re-heat them briefly in a warming oven.

# White Corn Muffins with Green Chilies

Vertamae Grosvenor                                    Makes 12 muffins

I have found that sometimes people want more than one corn muffin, but 2 muffins are too many. So I often use pans with miniature muffin cups. That way diners can eat 4 or 5 muffins without any problem. For a yummy variation, add 1/4 cup white corn kernels to the batter with the chilies.

2 cups white cornmeal

1 tablespoon baking powder

1 teaspoon salt

½ teaspoon baking soda

2 eggs

1 cup milk

¼ cup corn oil

½ cup well-drained canned chopped green chilies

Preheat an oven to 450 degrees F. Liberally grease a standard 12-cup muffin tin.

In a medium bowl, stir together the cornmeal, baking powder, salt, and baking soda. In a large bowl, beat the eggs until blended, then stir in the milk, corn oil, and chilies. Add the cornmeal mixture and stir just until there are no lumps; do not overmix.

Pour the batter into the prepared muffin tin, dividing it evenly among the cups and filling each cup about two-thirds full. Bake until risen and golden on top, 15 to 20 minutes.

Remove from the oven and let cool for a few minutes before turning the muffins out of the tin. If necessary, ease them out with the tip of a sharp knife.

# Irish Soda Bread

Mollie Katzen                                    Makes 1 10-inch round panful

For a superb variation on this quick and easy bread, try substituting oat and barley flours for the whole wheat and white. Buy them in a natural food store, or grind rolled oats and pearl barley in a blender or food processor. Bring this one to the table fresh from the oven.

2 cups whole wheat flour

2 cups unbleached white flour

3 teaspoons baking powder

2 teaspoon baking soda

2 tablespoons brown sugar

1 teaspoon salt

¼ cup melted butter

2 eggs

1⅓ cups yogurt

Golden raisins or currants (optional)

1 teaspoon caraway seeds (optional)

¼ cup poppy seeds (optional)

Preheat oven to 375° (350° for a glass pan). Butter a 10-inch round pan.

In a large bowl, sift together flours, baking powder, baking soda, sugar, and salt.

Beat together melted butter, eggs, and yogurt.

Make a well in the center of the dry ingredients, and stir in the wet ingredients. Mix briefly until reasonably well blended. (The batter does not need to be elegant.)

Add optional touches (raisins or currants and/or seeds)—or not.

Spoon dough into the prepared pan, then spread as evenly as possible. Shape it into a smooth mound, higher in the middle, tapered on the sides.

Bake 40 to 50 minutes—until a knife inserted all the way into the center comes out clean. The top will be quite brown.

Cool for 10 minutes, then remove from the pan. It may be served hot, cut into wedges, and wrapped in a clean tea towel in a big bowl. This bread is delicious warm, and is also very good at room temperature or cold.

# Chipotle Cheese Bread

Barbara Pool Fenzl

Makes 2 loaves

**Jalapeños are probably the most popular chile in the Southwest. This bread contains both the fresh and the dried, smoked version called chipotles. The cheese counteracts some of the heat from the chiles and adds great flavor. Spread with a flavored butter and serve with your favorite soup or salad. It's also a great sandwich bread, stuffed with smoked turkey, chile-sparked mayonnaise, Monterey jack cheese, avocado, tomatoes, and sprouts.**

1 package active dry yeast

¼ cup plus 1 teaspoon sugar

2 cups warm water (100° to 110°)

5 to 6 cups unbleached all-purpose flour

2 teaspoons salt

1 teaspoon ground cinnamon

2 jalapeño chiles, finely diced

1 cup Monterey jack cheese

2 chipotle chiles in adobo sauce, puréed and strained

In a bowl, stir together the yeast, 1 teaspoon of the sugar, and the water. Allow to sit for 5 minutes until the yeast is foamy.

In the bowl of an electric mixer or in a large bowl, stir together 5 cups of the flour, the remaining ¼ cup sugar, salt, and cinnamon; add the jalapeños and the cheese. Add the yeast-water mixture and the chipotle purée and mix well, either by hand or with the dough hook of the mixer. The dough should be soft; add more flour if necessary. If kneading by hand, turn the dough out onto a floured board and knead until the dough is smooth and elastic, about 10 minutes. If kneading in the mixer, knead until the dough pulls away from the side of the bowl and is smooth and elastic, about 5 minutes. Place the dough in a large, lightly oiled bowl, cover with a clean kitchen towel or plastic wrap, and set aside to rise in a warm place. Let rise until doubled, about 1 hour.

Punch the dough down and, with floured hands, shape into two oblong loaves. Place the loaves on a parchment paper-lined baking sheet and place in a warm place to rise. Let rise until doubled, 45 minutes to 1 hour.

Preheat an oven to 400°. With a sharp knife, cut ½-inch-deep slashes about 2 inches apart along the length of the loaves. Place a baking sheet in the center of the hot oven and bake until the loaves are lightly browned and sound hollow when tapped, 25 to 30 minutes. Remove from the oven and transfer the loaves to a cooling rack.

# Small Light Country Loaves

Jacques Pépin                                    Makes 4 loaves

**A favorite at my house, this is bread like you find in the French countryside—airy (with large holes inside) and full of flavor. The dough is extremely soft and so is not worked by hand until after the second proofing, when it is formed into a ball, divided into four pieces, and placed on a lined baking pan. The bread and liner then are slid out of the pan and onto a bread stone for baking. The 2 teaspoons of yeast in the recipe can be reduced to 1 1/2 or even 1 teaspoon in full summer or in areas where there is great humidity, as yeast develops more rapidly and gives you more extending power in these conditions.**

4 cups all-purpose flour (1 pound, 5 ounces), with 1 tablespoon reserved for dusting the tops of the loaves

2 teaspoons instant granulated yeast

2 teaspoons salt

2 cups cool water

## A Variation: Small Light Country Loaves with Mixed Grains

½ cup mixed grains (see note, below)

2 tablespoons water

To the original recipe ingredients, add the mixed grains and 2 tablespoons of water. Proceed as instructed in the original recipe.

*Note: Mixtures of up to 10 grains —including oats, millet, bulgur, etc.— can be purchased at most supermarkets. Or, you can choose an assortment of your favorite grains at a health food store for use in this recipe.*

Place all bread dough ingredients in the bowl of a food processor, and process the mixture for 15 seconds.

Transfer the dough to a bowl, cover it with plastic wrap, and let it rise for about 3½ hours at room temperature (60 to 70 degrees).

Release the dough from the sides of the bowl with your fingers, and press it firmly into the center of the bowl, repeating this procedure until all the dough is deflated and in a ball again.

Cover the dough again with plastic wrap, and let it rise for 2 hours. Then deflate the dough as described in the previous step, and form it into a ball. Moisten you hands, and break the dough into 4 pieces of about equal size.

Arrange the pieces of dough so they are equally spaced on a cookie sheet lined with parchment paper or a nonstick baking mat. Moisten your hands again, and press on the dough pieces to flatten them. Place an inverted roasting pan over the cookie

sheet to simulate a proof box and so prevent the dough from crusting on top as it rises. Let the dough rise for 45 minutes.

Meanwhile, preheat an oven with a bread stone in the center rack to 425 degrees.

After the dough has risen for 45 minutes, remove the roasting pan, and dust the tops of the loaves with the reserved flour. Firmly holding the sides of the liner, slide it and the loaves carefully onto the hot bread stone. Using a spray bottle filled with tap water, mist the interior of the oven a few times, then quickly close the door to create steam. Repeat this misting process after 2 or 3 minutes, and bake the bread for a total of 35 to 40 minutes.

Slide the loaves and liner onto a wire rack. Let the loaves cool for 10 to 15 minutes, then remove the liner. Continue to cool the loaves on the rack until they are at room temperature.

# Green Onion Cakes

Martin Yan
Makes 12

**These unleavened fried breads are thin and flat, crispy on the outside, moist and chewy inside and bursting with oniony flavor. I like to serve them the traditional way, as the street vendors do: sliced in wedges and eaten out of hand, plain or with a spicy chili-garlic dipping sauce.**

### Dough

3⅓ cups all-purpose flour

1¼ cups warm water

¼ cup shortening or cooking oil

2 teaspoons sesame oil

1 cup chopped green onions

2 teaspoons salt

½ teaspoon white pepper

### Dipping Sauce

½ cup chicken broth

2 tablespoons soy sauce

2 teaspoons chopped green onions

1 teaspoon minced garlic

1 teaspoon chili sauce

Cooking oil for pan-frying

Place flour in a bowl. Add water, stirring with chopsticks or a fork, until dough holds together. On a lightly floured board, knead dough until smooth and satiny, about 5 minutes. Cover and let rest for 30 minutes.

Combine dipping sauce ingredients in a bowl; set aside.

On a lightly floured board, roll dough into a cylinder, then cut into 12 portions. To make each cake, roll a portion of dough to make an 8-inch circle about ⅛-inch thick; keep remaining dough covered to prevent drying. Brush with shortening. Sprinkle sesame oil, green onions,

salt, and pepper on top. Roll dough into a cylinder and coil dough into a round patty; tuck end of dough underneath. Roll again to make an 8-inch circle about ⅛-inch thick.

Place a 10-inch frying pan over medium heat. Add 2 tablespoons oil, swirling to coat sides. Add a cake and cook until golden brown on each side, 2 to 3 minutes on each side. Remove and drain on paper towels. Add more oil as needed, swirling to coat sides. Repeat with remaining cakes.

Cut cakes into wedges and serve hot with dipping sauce on the side.

# Recipe Notes

**Bean Thread Noodles**
These Asian noodles, made from mung bean starch, are also called glass or cellophane noodles as they become transparent when rehydrated.

**Bell Peppers**
To core and seed: Slice off top and bottom ends. Lay the pepper on its side and slit open to form one long, flat strip. Set strip skin side down, then cut away ribs and seeds with a knife. To dice: Cut into strips, then cut crosswise into cubes.

**Black Bean Garlic Sauce**
This prepared Asian sauce, made from salted black beans, rice wine, and garlic, is added to stir-fries and sauces.

**Chiles**
Fresh chiles have a fiery compound in their ribs and seeds that can burn your eyes and face. Wear disposable gloves when handling them, and wash hands well when you're done. To dice: Cut flesh into strips, then cut the strips crosswise into small cubes. To roast: Hold the chile with tongs over a gas flame or set on a grill or under a hot broiler until the skin turns black. Place in a plastic or paper bag for 15 minutes. Rub off the skin, then remove and discard the stem and seeds.

**Chili Garlic Sauce**
This ready-to-use spicy Asian sauce is made from a blend of fresh and dried chiles and vinegar, plus garlic.

**Citrus**
To zest oranges, lemons, limes: Remove the thin colored skin (the zest) with the coarse teeth of a grater, or peel off threads of zest with a zester, then chop up with a knife. To juice: Ream lemons and limes with a wooden citrus juicer, or squeeze them by hand. An electric juicer does the best job with large oranges.

**Clarified Butter**
The clear yellow liquid that remains when butter is melted and the milk solids removed can withstand high heat without browning. To clarify: Melt butter over low heat or in the microwave. Carefully pour off and reserve the clear liquid; discard the milky residue. Clarified butter keeps in the refrigerator for several weeks.

**Galangal Powder**
This is the powdered form of a ginger-related rhizome used throughout Southeast Asia to season curry pastes, soups, and stews. Asian markets carry it (sometimes under its Indonesian name "laos" or "laos powder").

**Garam Masala**
A pantry staple in India, this seasoning blend often includes such "warm" spices as cardamom, black peppercorns, cloves, cumin, and cinnamon, but the mix often varies by region and by cook. Look for it in Indian markets.

## Julienne

Both the technique—to cut food like matchsticks—and the matchstick-shaped food that results are called julienne. To julienne: Cut food into thin slices ($\frac{1}{8}$ to $\frac{1}{4}$ inch) with a sharp knife. Stack the slices and cut them lengthwise into strips (of the same thickness), then again crosswise to desired lengths.

## Fish Sauce

Distinctly pungent and salty, this thin, brown fermented fish extract is a staple flavoring agent throughout Southeast Asia and southern China.

## Lemongrass

A long, pencil-thin herb, lemongrass infuses Southeast Asian foods with a delicate lemony flavor and aroma.

## Mango

To peel, pit, chop: Stand the fruit on its broad bottom. Slice top to bottom about $\frac{1}{2}$ inch away from its midsection on both sides. Score the flesh into squares, then slice off as cubes with a paring knife.

## Oyster-Flavored Sauce

This thick, dark-brown versatile Asian seasoning is made from oyster extracts and seasonings. It lends a distinct sweet-smoky flavor to stir-fries.

## Shrimp

To shell: Pull open the paper-thin shell along the underside of the shrimp, then carefully peel it away. To devein: Run the tip of a small knife along the top of the shrimp, then lift up and remove the black vein.

## Sesame Oil

Pressed from toasted sesame seeds, this dark amber oil is a much-appreciated flavoring agent for its nutty taste and aroma. Use in small amounts in stir-fries, marinades, and dressings.

## Toasting Nuts

Arrange nuts in a single layer on a baking sheet and bake at 350 degrees until fragrant and slightly brown, about 5 to 7 minutes.

## Tomato

To peel: Cut an X in the bottom of the tomato and drop in boiling water until skin starts to peel away, 1 to 2 minutes. Place in cold water, then peel off the skin when cool enough to handle. To seed: Halve across the middle. Squeeze each half (over a bowl or the sink) to pop out the seeds. To dice: Cut in $\frac{1}{4}$-inch slices. Stack the slices, and cut in $\frac{1}{4}$-inch strips. Cut strips crosswise into $\frac{1}{4}$-inch cubes.

# *Chefs*

**Marcia Adams**

An authority on Amish foods and folk-ways, Marcia Adams also writes with equal knowledge about Midwestern and American cuisine. She has just finished her sixth cookbook, *New Recipes from Quilt Country*, which is the companion book for her latest public television series, *Marcia Adams: More Cooking from Quilt Country*.

Photo by Tom Galliher

**Lidia Matticchio Bastianich**

Italian-born Lidia Bastianich came to America at age twelve. In 1981 she and her husband, Felice, opened Felidia, which would quickly become one of the nation's top-ranked Italian restaurants, in New York City. In *Lidia's Italian Table* she shows viewers how to replicate her intensely flavorful cooking style.

Photo by Amos Chan

**Brennan's and Executive Chef Michael Roussel**

A culinary phenomenon since 1946, Brennan's Restaurant in New Orleans has created some of the world's most famous dishes. Founder Owen Edward Brennan was the culinary renaissance man of his time and today the Brennan name is synonymous with fine dining. As host of public television's *Breakfast in New Orleans*, Brennan's executive chef, Michael Roussel, shares the family's gastronomic secrets.

Photo © Brennan's Restaurant

**Giuliano Bugialli**

The tempting Italian cuisine of Giuliano Bugialli tantalizes the American palate while nurturing our appreciation of its tradition. Giuliano shares his passion for his country and *la cucina italiana* in his first public television series, *Bugialli's Italy*. As always, he serves up something new—unusual and engaging regional recipes along with the history, tradition, and techniques that bring them to life.

Photo by John Dominis

**Julia Child**

America's best beloved television cook is Julia Child. Her students are middle-class Americans and her lesson is "you can do it." She calls herself a home cook and she has no pretensions about her passion: good food. Everyone has a warm memory of a classic "Julia" moment and we all look forward to whatever she cooks up next.

Photo by Michael P. McLaughlin

**Nathalie Dupree**

Although Nathalie Dupree trained at London's Cordon Bleu, her heart always belonged to the South. A long-time Georgia resident, she founded Rich's Cooking School in Atlanta before launching one of the most enduring cooking show careers in public television. In her latest series, *Nathalie Dupree Entertains*, she teaches us that cooking and entertaining should be fun and relaxing.

Photo by Tess Conway

**Todd English**
Internationally acclaimed chef and restaurateur Todd English grew up in an Italian family that took their food seriously. Today, known for his unique interpretive European cuisine, Todd brings his high-style culinary techniques and recipes into the average cook's home kitchen through his public television series, *Cooking In with Todd English*.
Photo by Carl Tremblay

**Mary Ann Esposito**
Creator and host of *Ciao Italia*, Mary Ann Esposito grew up in Buffalo, New York, where the kitchen was the heart and soul of her family's home. She has been serving up *Ciao Italia* on public television since 1989, when she piqued the nation's interest in an Italian cooking show seasoned with cultural tidbits.
Photo by Bill Truslow Photography

**Barbara Pool Fenzl**
A major figure on the culinary stage, Barbara Pool Fenzl has helped bring Southwestern cuisine to America's table. Barbara's first love is teaching and her technique shines as host of public television's *Savor the Southwest*. She is also a renowned cookbook author and owner of the prestigious Les Gourmettes Cooking School in Phoenix.
Photo by Jorgen Larson

**Debbi Fields**
At twenty-two, and without any prior business experience, Debbi Fields opened her first chocolate chip-cookie store. Seven hundred stores and three cookbooks later, the now famous "Mrs. Fields" hosts public television's *Debbi Fields' Great American Desserts*. This treat-making entrepreneur inspires cooks and bakers everywhere to create and indulge in her sinfully satisfying delights at home.
Photo courtesy Mrs. Fields

**Lynn Fischer**
The quick rise of Lynn Fischer from obscurity to a nationally recognized health expert was spurred by her husband's dangerously high cholesterol count. Determined to cure his heart disease through diet, she began a journey that taught her the importance of lowfat living. Today, her husband enjoys better health and we all can benefit from Lynn's experience on her public television series, *Healthy Indulgences*.
Photo courtesy St. Martin's Press

**John D. Folse**
Chef John Folse is an authority on Cajun and Creole cuisine and culture. He hosts public television's *A Taste of Louisiana*, now in it's seventh season. A native son of his beloved Bayou State, John knows Louisiana is filled with color and tradition as well as folks who love a good time as much as they love great food.
Photo by Jose Garcia

### Pierre Franey

Pierre Franey's passion for French cooking is legendary. From his famed French restaurants' haute-cuisine feasts to his popular television series *Cuisine Rapide* and *The New York Times* column "60-Minute Gourmet" he did much to bring French cooking to America. His sweet smile and charming style easily won the heart of the American cook and led to several best-selling cookbooks and his award-winning public television series, *Pierre Franey's Cooking in France*. Pierre Franey passed away in October 1996 at the age of seventy-five, just after teaching a cooking class on the Queen Elizabeth 2.
Photo by Martin Brigdale

### Vertamae Grosvenor

Storyteller, poet, and culinary anthropologist Vertamae Grosvenor has been exploring and sharing the roots of culinary culture for more than twenty-five years. Vertamae learned to cook in the South Carolina Lowcountry and, as host of public television's *The Americas' Family Kitchen with Vertamae Grosvenor*, she continues to share her passion for food.
Photo by Gary Hannarbarge

### George Hirsch

With great determination, George Hirsch worked his way up through the culinary ranks from washing dishes to graduating with honors from the Culinary Institute of America. His public television series, *Know Your Fire*, helps home cooks get the most out of their grills year-round.
Photo by Dan Kossoff

### Madhur Jaffrey

Born in Delhi, India, Madhur Jaffrey shares her culinary discoveries in her public television series, *Flavors of India*. In Madhur's recipes the reader has an exceptional opportunity: to share the best beloved foods of that exotic nation in a gastronomic tour.

### Madeleine Kamman

Born in Paris, Madeleine Kamman discovered her love of food at an early age with her grandmother's, mother's, and great-aunts' cooking at her family home. Today, she uses the techniques of her homeland with American ingredients to create culinary triumphs. She is an acclaimed restaurateur, instructor, and author of seven cookbooks including *Madeleine Cooks*, companion book to her public television series.
Photo © William Morrow & Company, Inc.

### Mollie Katzen

Cookbook author and artist Mollie Katzen helped bring vegetarian cooking from the fringes of American society to mainstream dinner tables. Her *Moosewood Cookbook*, first published in 1972, was at the forefront of the revolution in vegetarian cuisine. She continues to inspire and influence America's palate through her public television series, *Mollie Katzen's Cooking Show*.
Photo by Lisa Keating

### Graham Kerr

Since 1959, Graham Kerr has entertained and educated generations of home cooks. Now, more than ever, he is combining his message of healthful cooking with the need to make mealtimes as fun, creative, and satisfying as they are nourishing. He is author of twenty-three books. His latest, *The Gathering Place*, is also the companion book to his new television series.

Photo © The Kerr Corporation

### Efrain Martinez, Chef Ef

"Chef Ef" is the nom de cuisine of Efrain Martinez on public television's *Classic Spanish Cooking with Chef Ef*. Former owner of La Posada, the first Spanish restaurant in New York's Hudson Valley region, Chef Ef's life work is to introduce Spanish cuisine to American audiences.

Photo by Anthony Passarotti

### Joan Nathan

Nationally acclaimed cookbook author Joan Nathan is host and executive producer of the public television series, *Jewish Cooking in America with Joan Nathan*. Joan uses food to explore Jewish culture and history in the United States. Her programs highlight the integral role of food in binding family and community throughout the generations.

Photo © Michael P. McLaughlin

### Jennifer Paterson and Clarissa Dickson Wright, Two Fat Ladies

Large, loud, and proud of their good old-fashioned cooking, the Two Fat Ladies (Jennifer Paterson and Clarissa Dickson Wright) came direct from the BBC to win American's hearts with their delightfully decadent meals and legendary attitudes. These pleasingly plump ladies have been splendid kitchen companions and hosts of their own public television series, *Two Fat Ladies*. Jennifer Patterson passed away in August 1999.

Photo © BBC. Photographer: Jason Bell

### Caprial Pence

One of the rising young stars of public television, Caprial Pence brings simple elegance to American comfort food and cultural specialties with her series, *Cooking with Caprial: American Bistro Fare*. Caprial's warmth and candor encourages busy people who want a meal that is delicious yet looks like it was prepared by a master.

Photo by Jerome Hart

### Jacques Pépin

Born into a restaurant family in Bourg-en-Bresse, France, Jacques Pépin worked in acclaimed restaurants and served as personal chef to three French heads of state before coming to America in 1959. One of the nation's foremost cooking teachers, Jacques has used his many public television cooking shows to demonstrate the importance of good technique.

Photo by Thomas Heinz

### Paul Prudhomme

The name Paul Prudhomme is synonymous with Louisiana cuisine. Paul grew up in bayou country in a house without electricity, where the family depended on nature's bounty for sustenance. In 1979 he opened K-Paul's Louisiana Kitchen in New Orleans, which led to worldwide acclaim. In his latest series, *Kitchen Expedition*, he shares recipes from his global gastronomic adventures.
Photo by Paul Rico

### Stephan Pyles

Texas-born Stephan Pyles began cooking at his family's truckstop when he was eight. Today *Bon Appétit* magazine says he is "almost single-handedly changing the cooking scene in Texas." As host of *New Tastes from Texas*, he mixes a dash of cowboy with a pinch of Southern, Latin, and Southwestern to create his taste-tempting innovations.
Photo by Ben Fink

### John Shields

Known as the "Culinary Ambassador of the Chesapeake Bay," John Shields is a nationally acclaimed chef and an expert in Chesapeake cuisine. In his public television series, *Chesapeake Bay Cooking with John Shields*, he shares his passion for the region and celebrates its culinary treasures, lore, and history.
Photo by Susan Noonan

### Rick Stein

Britain's Rick Stein is the exuberant host of the public television series *Rick Stein's Fruits of the Sea*. Rick dispels myths about preparing and enjoying seafood at home while taking viewers on savory local excursions to share in his simple reverence for the ocean off Cornwall and its seafaring people.
Photo by Laurie Evans

### Nick Stellino

In Nick Stellino's loving and colorful Sicilian family, love and food were irrevocably linked. Today, due to his passion for cooking, he hosts *Cucina Amore*. Nick's infectious enthusiasm, the trattoria setting, and the irresistible cuisine have quickly made this show one of the most popular on public television.
Photo by E.J. Armstrong

### Tommy Tang

Born in Bangkok, Tommy Tang immigrated to the United States in 1972. Once landed, he began a culinary adventure that led to owning bi-coastal restaurants and developing his own line of Thai spices. His public television cooking series, *Tommy Tang's Modern Thai Cuisine*, is shot on location in Thailand and considered irreverent, inspirational, flamboyant, and fun.
Photo courtesy WMHT Educational Telecommunications

**Jacques Torres**
In Provence, where he grew up, Jacques Torres began baking at an early age. In 1980, on a bet with a friend, he started a career that led to his becoming the youngest recipient of the Meilleur Ouvrier de France Pâtissier award. As host of public television's *Dessert Circus*, he shares his passion for the art of pastry.
Photo by Lou Manna

**Charlie Trotter**
After a decade of practicing his art, Charlie Trotter clearly established himself as a true visionary of modem American cuisine. His "dream restaurant" became a reality and an instant success in 1987 when he opened Charlie Trotter's in Chicago. Now, he shares his culinary vision on public television's *The Kitchen Sessions with Charlie Trotter*.
Photo by Paul Elledge

**Joanne Weir**
Host of *Weir Cooking in the Wine Country*, Joanne Weir is a fourth-generation professional cook. Joanne's great-grandmother operated a restaurant in Boston at the turn of the century and started a family tradition of culinary excellence. Today, Joanne brings her own warmth and enthusiasm to her cookbooks, articles, and television programs.
Photo by Kim Steele

**Burt Wolf**
Host and author Burt Wolf has six internationally syndicated television series that deal with food, travel, and cultural history to his credit. He was the first recipient of the James Beard Foundation Award for "Best Television Food Journalism." In *Burt Wolf Travels and Traditions* he travels to cities around the world and tells the stories of local traditions that have influenced the entire world.
Photo by Emily Aronson

**Roy Yamaguchi**
Many people say that Roy Yamaguchi is Hawaii's best-known chef. He adheres to the home-grown philosophy of Hawaiian cuisine, yet he has crafted a distinctive culinary style that has earned worldwide fame and recognition. His public television series, *Hawaii Cooks with Roy Yamaguchi*, showcases the diversity of Hawaii's land, people, and culture.
Photo by Rae Huo

**Martin Yan**
America's foremost Chinese chef, Martin Yan, has been wowing TV audiences with his lightening cleaver skills since 1982—making his *Yan Can Cook* series one of the longest-running hits on public television. His flashy knife work and natural showmanship on camera belie decades of serious culinary training in Hong Kong, Canada, and the United States.
Photo by Geoffrey Nilsen

# Credits

**Marcia Adams**
Pages 39 and 113 are from Marcia Adams *New Recipes from Quilt Country* by Marcia Adams. Copyright © 1997 by Marcia Adams. Reprinted by permission of Clarkson N. Potter/Publishers, a division of Random House, Inc.

**Lidia Matticchio Bastianich**
Page 119 is from *Lidia's Italian Table* by Lidia Matticchio Bastianich. Copyright © 1998 by Lidia Matticchio Bastianich. Reprinted by permission of William Morrow & Company, Inc.

**Brennan's**
Pages 98 and 131 are from *Breakfast at Brennan's and Dinner, Too* by Brennan's, Pip, Jimmy, and Ted Brennan. Copyright © 1994 by Brennan's Inc. Reprinted by permission of Brennan's.

**Guiliano Bugialli**
Pages 46 and 84 are from *Bugialli's Italy* by Guiliano Bugialli. Copyright © 1998 by Giuliano Bugialli. Reprinted by permission of William Morrow & Company, Inc.

**Julia Child**
Pages 30 and 67 are from *The Way to Cook* by Julia Child. Copyright © 1989 by Julia Child. Reprinted by permission of Alfred A. Knopf, Inc.

**Nathalie Dupree**
Pages 22 and 116 are from *Nathalie Dupree's Comfortable Entertaining* by Nathalie Dupree. Copyright © 1998 by Nathalie Dupree. Used by permission of Viking Penguin, a division of Penguin Putnam Inc. Photo page 117 © Tom Eckerle.

**Todd English**
Pages 62, 71, and 125 are from *Cooking in With Todd English* by Todd English. Copyright © 1998 CPTV. Reprinted by permission of CPTV (Connecticut Public Television).

**Mary Ann Esposito**
Page 49 is from *Mangia Pasta!* by Mary Ann Esposito. Copyright © 1998 Mary Ann Esposito. Reprinted by permission of William Morrow & Company, Inc.

**Barbara Pool Fenzl**
Pages 33, 52, 61, 112, and 146 are from *Savor the Southwest* by Barbara Pool Fenzl with Jane Horn. Copyright © 1999 by Arizona Board of Regents. Photographs copyright © Frankie Frankeny. Reprinted by permission of Bay Books & Tapes Inc. Photos pages 32, 53, and 112 by Frankie Frankeny.

**Debbi Fields**
Pages 126 and 130 reprinted with the permission of Simon & Schuster, Inc. from *Great American Desserts* by Debra J. Fields. Copyright © 1996 by Debra J. Fields and Reid/Land Productions.

**Lynn Fischer**
Pages 28, 54, 60, and 108 are from *Healthy Indulgences* by Lynn Fischer. Copyright © 1995 by Lynn Fischer. Reprinted by permission of William Morrow & Company, Inc.

**John D. Folse**
Pages 36, 73, and 127 are from *Chef John Folse's Louisiana Sampler* by Chef John D. Folse. Copyright © 1996 by Chef John D. Folse, CEC, AAC. Reprinted by permission of Chef John Folse & Company Publishing.

**Pierre Franey**
Pages 76, 109, and 142 are from *Pierre Franey's Cooking in France* by Pierre Franey and Richard Flaste. Copyright © 1994 by Pierre Franey and Richard Flaste. Reprinted by permission of Alfred A. Knopf, Inc.

**Vertamae Grosvenor**
Pages 51, 89, and 145 are from *Vertamae Cooks in the Americas Family Kitchen* by Vertamae Grosvenor. Copyright © 1996 by Window to the World Communications, More Than Equal Productions, and Vertamae Grosvenor. Reprinted by permission of Bay Books & Tapes, Inc. Photos pages 50, 88, and 144 by Joyce Oudkerk Pool.

**George Hirsch**
Pages 76, 86, and 99 are from *Grilling with Chef George Hirsch* by George Hirsch with Marie Bianco. Copyright © 1994 by George Hirsch. Reprinted by permission of Hearst Books.

**Madhur Jaffrey**
Page 143 was reprinted from *Madhur Jaffrey's Flavors of India*, copyright © 1995 by Madhur Jaffrey, which was published to accompany the television series "Great Food" courtesy of West 175 Enterprises Inc./BBC Worldwide.

**Madeleine Kamman**
Pages 28, 80, and 139 are from *Madeleine Cooks* by Madeleine Kamman. Copyright © 1986 by Baffico/Breger Video, Inc. Reprinted by permission of William Morrow and Company, Inc.

**Mollie Katzen**
Pages 31, 55, and 145 are reprinted with permission from *Still Life with Menu Cookbook*. Copyright © 1988 by Mollie Katzen, Ten Speed Press, PO Box 7123, Berkeley, California 94707. Available from your local bookseller or call 800-841-2665, or visit our website at www.tenspeed.com.

# Index

**AN AMERICAN FEAST**